Health risks to the health care professional

Edited by

Paul Lichfield MB FFOM

Director of Medical Services,
Civil Service Occupational Health Service

ROYAL COLLEGE OF PHYSICIANS OF LONDON
in association with the
FACULTY OF OCCUPATIONAL MEDICINE

1995

Acknowledgements

The Royal College of Physicians acknowledges with thanks a grant from the Department of Health towards the cost of producing this book.

Royal College of Physicians of London
11 St Andrews Place, London NW1 4LE

Registered Charity No. 210508

Copyright © 1995 Royal College of Physicians of London
ISBN 1 873240 95 3

Typeset by Dan-Set Graphics, Telford, Shropshire
Printed in Great Britain by Cathedral Print Services Ltd, Salisbury

Foreword

The Royal College of Physicians and the Faculty of Occupational Medicine have been concerned for some time that the National Health Service has hitherto made scant provision to protect the mental and physical health of its own workforce; although, it must be said, most health care professionals have little thought that they themselves might some day be in need of care and protection at their place of work. But in the last few years the hazards of a fast moving, increasingly complex technological industry, together with the rapid changes in the structure and function of the NHS have accentuated the need for an effective and efficient occupational health service for the NHS itself.

This report of a meeting arranged by the College and the Faculty draws attention to the areas where the risks are greatest and the steps that can be taken by managers and health care professionals themselves to reduce these risks and provide adequate support at their place of work for those who need it.

Leslie Turnberg
President of the Royal College of Physicians

Ewan B Macdonald
Dean of the Faculty of Occupational Medicine

August 1995

Contributors

David Baldwin MB BS MRCPsych *Senior Lecturer in Psychiatry and Consultant in General and Community Psychiatry, University of Southampton and Royal South Hants Hospital, Graham Road, Southampton SO14 0YG; formerly: Consultant Psychiatrist, John Conolly Wing, West London Healthcare NHS Trust, Uxbridge Road, Southall, Middlesex UB1 3EU*

Anne Cockcroft MD FRCP FFOM *Consultant and Senior Lecturer in Occupational Medicine, Royal Free Hampstead NHS Trust and Royal Free Hospital School of Medicine, Occupational Health Unit, 5 Rosslyn Hill, Hampstead, London NW3 5UL*

Geoffrey M Dusheiko MB FRCP FCP(SA) *Reader in Medicine and Honorary Consultant Physician, Royal Free Hospital School of Medicine and Royal Free Hampstead NHS Trust, Rowland Hill Street, London NW3 2PF*

Christopher C Harling MA FRCP FFOM *Consultant and Clinical Lecturer in Occupational Medicine, United Bristol Healthcare NHS Trust and the University of Bristol, Department of Health & Safety, Bristol Royal Infirmary, Bristol BS2 8HW*

Roger Higgs MBE FRCP FRCGP *Professor and Head of Department of General Practice and Primary Care, King's College School of Medicine and Dentistry, Bessemer Road, London SE5 9PJ*

Rachel Jenkins MD MRCPsych *Principal Medical Officer, Health Care (Medical), Mental Health, Elderly, Disability and Ethics Policy Branch, Department of Health, Wellington House, 133–155 Waterloo Road, London SE1 8UG*

Desmond Kelly MD FRCP FRCPsych *Visiting Professor at University College London and Medical Director, The Priory Hospital, Priory Lane, Roehampton, London SW15 5JJ*

Elizabeth C McCloy MB BS FRCP FFOM *Chief Executive and Director, Civil Service Occupational Health Service, 18–20 Hill Street, Edinburgh EH2 3NB*

Steve McKeown MB BS MRCPsych *Clinical Director, Cheadle Royal Health Care Services, Masters House, Bexton Road, Knutsford, Cheshire WA16 0BU*

Anthony J Newman Taylor OBE FRCP FFOM *Consultant Physician, Royal Brompton Hospital, and Professor of Occupational & Environmental Medicine, National Heart & Lung Institute, Department of Occupational & Environmental Medicine, 1b Manresa Road, London SW3 6LR*

David W Rees DIPCLINPSYCH PhD *Director of Psychology Services. Department of Clinical Psychology, North Manchester Healthcare NHS Trust, Delaunays Road, Crumpsalll, Manchester M8 6RL*

Shauna E Rudge MB BS MRCPsych *Senior Registrar in Psychiatry, John Conolly Wing, West London Healthcare NHS Trust, Uxbridge Road, Southall, Middlesex UB1 3EU*

Craig Skinner MB ChB FRCP *Consultant Physician and Senior Clinical Lecturer in Medicine, Heartlands Hospital and Chest Clinic, Birmingham and the University of Birmingham. Bordesley Green East, Birmingham B9 5ST*

Contents

Editor's introduction

The health care sector is a major part of the UK economy accounting for some 6.9% of GDP in 1994. Well over one million people work in the National Health Service (NHS), which is widely acknowledged as being the largest employer in Europe, but until recently there has only been patchy management interest in the health of NHS staff. Occupational health services have been slow to develop in much of the NHS and the advice of occupational health departments is still often undervalued by fellow health care professionals. Most large employers in the UK closely monitor the health of their workforce and actively promote wellbeing but such good practice is uncommon in the health care industry. Is this a case of the cobbler's children being poorly shod or is it, perhaps, an indication that health care is a low risk business?

There is certainly no lack of hazards in the clinical setting. Hospitals are large industrial sites within which a wide range of hazardous activities are carried out. Manual handling is an everyday activity for most nurses and physiotherapists while radiographers are potentially exposed to ionising radiation and ultrasound on a daily basis. Laboratory technicians deal with a number of hazardous chemicals and theatre staff use a variety of sharp implements in an environment which combines noxious gases and slippery floors with biohazards. Both hospital and community health care workers are increasingly exposed to the threat of physical violence and all are expected to come into contact with a range of infections as a condition of employment.

The modern approach to health and safety practice relies upon risk assessment and this has been codified within European and UK legislation. Once hazards are identified the risk of a given work practice resulting in harm should be assessed so that appropriate control measures can be instituted. In the health care industry not only are the hazards multivaried but the risks can be significant, although most elements of clinical care vary as a function of the individual patient which renders risk assessment problematical. Treatment regimes are frequently revised, requiring adaptation by staff and a reassessment of hazards and risks; this is often perceived as a low priority by those instituting the changes. Even if processes do remain constant, at least in the hospital setting, there is a high staff turnover with the consequent danger of lack of awareness of hazards and the potential corruption of verbally transmitted instructions. Attitudes can also militate against safe systems of work in that health care professionals, perhaps as the result of regular exposure to illness and injury, sometimes develop delusions of invulnerability and recklessly neglect their own health and welfare.

So the hazards are real, the risks can be significant and the development of health and safety countermeasures may have lagged behind industry best practice — but are matters improving? Certainly there has been an increasing awareness, at the centre, of the importance of occupational health provision within the NHS, and the Secretary of State has recently reinforced this personally. The number of consultant occupational physicians employed within the NHS has also risen greatly in recent years and only a minority of hospital staff are now served by departments employing doctors and/or nurses without higher specialist qualifications in occupational health. However, the great majority of those working in primary care still lack a formal source of occupational health and safety advice, and the NHS reforms are, in some cases, jeopardising established occupational health services by shifting their focus from the care of trust staff to income generation. Furthermore, although many hazards have been effectively controlled, there is an increasing awareness that viral agents, allergens and resistant strains of bacteria can represent a very real threat to the health of health carers.

The potential psychological harm that can result from the pressures of working in the medical field has been recognised for many years but the true scale of mental health problems is only now becoming apparent. Mental ill-health accounts for some 30% of all sickness absence, and work stress is a significant factor in many cases; excessive working hours, the introduction of new technology and organisational change are both prime stressors and characteristic features of the modern NHS.

The perception that health care is an industry in which health risks to employees may be both underestimated and poorly understood led the Royal College of Physicians to approach the Faculty of Occupational Medicine about a joint meeting to raise awareness. As a result a major conference was held at the Royal College of Physicians in London in 1994. The programme concentrated on the risks to physical and mental health, their identification and prevention. This published version of the proceedings has been edited and updated to take account of subsequent work but follows the same format with papers addressing, in the first half, the viral threat, tuberculosis and allergic respiratory disease and, in the second, burnout, depression and organisational stress. The final chapter, by Professor Roger Higgs and based on his Ernestine Henry Lecture, addresses the subject of creating a strategy for maintaining good mental health in health care work.

I am most grateful to all the contributors for agreeing to produce their texts in a form suitable for publication and then for updating, revising and proof-reading. Thanks are also due to Professor Humphrey Hodgson, College Academic Registrar, and to Doreen Miller, Faculty Registrar, for defining the need for this conference and then playing a major part in its organisation. Finally I would like to thank Philada Dann and Diana Beaven of the College Publications Department for their tireless enthusiasm in keeping up the momentum of this project and for their judicious but tactful prodding as various deadlines approached.

The cobbler's children may indeed be poorly shod but once the cobbler recognises the deficiency he has the wherewithal to remedy it. The NHS should be a shining example to the rest of industry of how to care for employees' health; though lack of resources will always be cited as an excuse for inaction, the main problem would often seem to be a fundamental failure of recognition. Education is the key to overcoming such a problem and I hope that, in some small way, the proceedings of this conference will help to extend our knowledge about the risks to their health faced by those who provide health care to others.

PAUL LITCHFIELD

July 1995

PART 1

Chemical and biological aspects

ELIZABETH C McCLOY
Chief Executive and Director,
Civil Service Occupational Health and Safety Agency

Chemical and biological agents are significant causes of occupationally acquired ill health in health care professionals. They also occupy opposite ends of the spectrum in the implementation of the hierarchical control of hazardous substances at work. The Control of Substances Hazardous to Health Regulations (COSHH) 1988 focused on the elimination of a hazardous substance as the ideal control mechanism. Failing that, substitution with a less hazardous substance, minimising exposure by enclosure, engineering design and exhaust ventilation are the preferred strategies.

The COSHH Regulations 1994 extend the previous guidance on the control of biological agents in the workplace and implement the recent European Directives on the protection of workers from risks related to exposure to biological agents at work (90/679/EEC) and the classification of biological agents (93/88/EEC). Schedule 9 of COSHH 1994 distinguishes between workplaces such as laboratories where employees are exposed to biological agents as an integral part of their work and those work activities where exposure is incidental to the main activity. 'Accidental' exposure, for example to respiratory tract infection, through normal social contact is excluded. Regulation 7 requires the employer so far as is reasonably practicable to prevent exposure by measures other than the provision of protective equipment except in the case of carcinogens and biological agents.

Hazard and risk are not synonymous. The hazard posed by a substance or biological agent is its potential to cause harm. Risk is a statistical concept—the probability or likelihood that harm will occur. As Dr Harling reminds us at the end of his chapter, HIV presents an extreme hazard to the health of health care workers (HCWs). The evidence suggests that the risk of that harm being manifest is comparatively low. Appreciation of the difference between hazard and risk is critical to the prevention and management of occupationally acquired disease.

Biological agents

Infections acquired by health care professionals through occupational transmission have been dominated for over 10 years by viral infections. 'What is the risk?' is the question posed most frequently by HCWs and is the one most difficult to answer. Dr Harling acknowledges the difficulty in quantifying the risk of occupational transmission of HIV infection. Worldwide, by May 1995 there had been 73 documented cases of occupational HIV transmission and 141 possible cases. The risk of occupationally acquired infection is estimated as 0.5%.

Dr Cockcroft reviews the evidence for an increased risk of occupationally acquired HBV infection in HCWs in hospitals and other HCWs employed in the general community. The probability of transmission is related to the antigen/antibody status of the carrier with the magnitude of risk ranging from 19–31% where the carrier is HBeAg positive to 1–6% where the carrier is HBeAg negative.

Serological tests for hepatitis C virus (HCV) have only been available since 1990. The first generation assays used in the early epidemiological studies of HCV infection in HCWs lacked sensitivity and specificity. Risk predictions based on that evidence are therefore unreliable. Later studies using second and third generation assays suggest that prevalence rates in HCWs are of the order of 2.0% and not significantly different from those in control populations. The attribution of HCV infection in HCWs to occupational cause is further complicated by the high percentage of community acquired infection. Although occupational transmission has been documented the overall risk of infection following needlestick injuries is 0–3%.

Transmission of viral infection from the HCW to patient is documented but uncommon. There is only one substantiated report of nosocomial transmission of HIV infection, from an infected Florida dentist to his patients. Dr Dusheiko refers to two anecdotal reports of transmission of HCV from surgeon to patient. The first case report of probable nosocomial HCV infection has recently been published.[1] However, transmission of HBV infection from HBeAg positive HCWs occurs more frequently and is linked with major surgical procedures deep in the body cavity without direct vision.

The worldwide increase in cases of TB during the late 1980s and 1990s, its association with HIV infection, the emergence of multiple drug resistant strains particularly in Asia, Africa and the USA has again brought this infection to the forefront of our attention. Dr Skinner defines risk activities for the HCW and places occupational risk for HCWs in the UK in perspective. The inappropriateness of routine pre-employment chest x-rays as a screening tool is emphasised. Following studies by NHS occupational health departments on the predictive value of tuberculin skin reactions in HCWs for active TB or x-ray abnormalities, chest x-rays should be reserved for those with suspicious symptoms.

Prevention

All risk control programmes must emphasise safe working practices including safe disposal of clinical waste and the use of personal protective equipment. They must also include post-exposure incident management plans. Where safe and effective vaccines exist, as for HBV, they should be an integral part of the risk control programme. Vaccination should be completed before exposure begins. The Department of Health has issued guidance on protecting health care workers and their patients from HBV. All HCWs who are involved in exposure prone procedures must be vaccinated against HBV and those who are HBeAg positive are excluded from undertaking these activities. HCWs who are HIV positive and HCWs who have been shown to be associated with transmission of HCV infection should no longer perform exposure prone procedures.

The lack of specific treatments for and vaccines against HIV and HCV has focused the attention of HCWs on the need to practise universal precautions and use appropriate personal protective equipment and clothing at all times. The management of occupational exposures must be undertaken by persons with up-to-date knowledge of the organisms that could potentially be transmitted. Dr Harling reminds us of the need to record all relevant details, some of which at the time may seem trivial compared with the distress of the individual HCW, and of the dangers of assuming that some HCWs by seniority or specialty automatically have knowledge of post-exposure procedures which could lead to avoidance of discussing, with tact and sympathy, issues such as blood/organ donation, sexual activity and pregnancy in the 6 month follow-up period.

Chemical agents

HCWs are at risk of acquiring occupational asthma. From January 1989 to December 1993 there were 107 cases of asthma in HCWs reported to SWORD—the Surveillance of Work and Occupational Respiratory Disease scheme. Establishing cause and effect for asthma resulting from chemicals such as formaldehyde and glutaraldehyde which are of low molecular weight may be difficult as evidence of specific IgE antibody is not often present. A good occupational history and the establishment of a clear-cut relationship between exposure and symptoms is essential. Although glutaraldehyde was the most common substance identified to SWORD, validation of the diagnosis by inhalation testing is infrequent. The suggestion has been made that the response is irritant rather than allergic.

Professor Newman Taylor rightly draws attention to the dramatic increase, particularly in the USA, in latex allergy in the past 5 years following the increased and widespread use of rubber gloves as an integral part of infection control procedures. However, in the UK, of the 107 cases of occupational asthma reported to SWORD only 6 were ascribed to latex/rubber gloves. He points out that latex allergy is of particular concern not only because of its ubiquitous use in the workplace but because of the high risk posed by exposure to latex and cross-reacting allergens in the general environment.

Awareness of the problem, knowledge as to how sensitisation is likely to occur, control of the work environment through effective exhaust ventilation and good work practice are particularly important control measures which if implemented effectively may reduce the incidence of occupational asthma in HCWs.

Reference

1. Communicable Disease Report. Hepatitis C virus transmission from health care worker to patient. *CDR Weekly* 1995; **5**(26): 30 June

1 | Human immunodeficiency virus

Christopher Harling
Consultant Occupational Physician, United Bristol Healthcare NHS Trust and Clinical Lecturer in Occupational Medicine, University of Bristol

---

The human immunodeficiency virus (HIV) is one of a group of bloodborne organisms that pose a risk to the health of health care professionals and share a number of common features. This chapter will look at the risks of occupational acquisition of HIV, strategies for the prevention of workplace infection and the management of occupational exposure.

Although HIV clearly represents a significant health hazard, quantifying the risk of infection in an occupational setting is more difficult. Anecdotal evidence of the possibility of occupational transmission appeared soon after the identification of HIV as the causative agent of AIDS,[1] but it was not until much later that epidemiological studies that included both numerator and denominator allowed an estimate of the risk of infection from a needlestick or other occupational injury to be calculated.

Risks of transmission

Surveillance programmes were set up in a number of countries, primarily in Europe and North America. World-wide, by the end of September 1993, it was reported[2] that 64 documented seroconversions following occupational exposure to HIV had been identified. In addition, a further 118 possible cases of occupational acquisition of HIV were recorded where the evidence was less convincing, though work-related incidents were still felt to be the most likely route of infection. These figures have subsequently increased to 67 documented occupational acquisitions and 123 possible cases by September 1994, though not all new cases for that period have yet been reported (K Porter, personal communication). For a case to be accepted as a definite occupational infection, the injured health care worker had to be shown to be HIV antibody negative at the time of the injury, with seroconversion at an appropriate time afterwards and no other risk factors for HIV infection.

A number of estimates of the risk of infection have been published, ranging from 0.18% to 5.8%. The rate reported in the UK study (2%) is based on less than 100 cases[2] and has a wide 95% confidence interval (0.3–7.1); the South African study[3] reports 52 accidental injuries with 3 seroconversions giving a rate of 5.8%. The other studies show rates of less than 1% and the figure generally quoted for risk analysis studies is 0.3%, which is included within the 95% confidence interval quoted for all the published studies.

The UK figures relate to prospective surveillance between 1985 and 1992;[2] of the injuries reported, 99 met the study criteria of exposure to known HIV infected blood or serum with baseline and 3 month post-exposure antibody tests available for the injured health care professional. Two of these injuries resulted in HIV seroconversion; it is reported that one of those injured had been treated with zidovudine after the accident. Two other cases of occupational acquisition that were not included within the surveillance programme are known to have occurred, giving a total of four occupationally acquired HIV infections in the UK.

Although these numbers are far too small to allow statistically robust conclusions to be drawn, a number of interesting points emerge. In all cases percutaneous exposure to blood was the originating incident and in all cases the procedure being undertaken was vessel puncture. In all four cases the source patient was a heterosexual female and in three of the four cases the HIV status of the source patient was known to the injured health care worker prior to the injury.

Prevention of injury

Turning now to the prevention of occupational transmission of HIV, it is clear from the reported studies that the major risk is a needlestick or similar injury that involves the percutaneous transmission of blood. Seroconversion has been reported after percutaneous injuries involving exposure to body fluids and mucocutaneous exposure to blood, particularly where the skin is not intact.[4] Accidents have also been reported from the USA[5] where there had been mucocutaneous or percutaneous exposure to concentrated viral fluid in laboratories followed by seroconversion. The main risk in numerical terms to health care professionals, however, remains percutaneous exposure to blood involving a hollow needle.

The prevention of occupational transmission of HIV requires a reduction in the rate of needlestick or other sharps injuries. The most important single preventive measure involves teaching all health care professionals about the safe handling of sharps and particularly the disposal of sharps and waste. It is simply unacceptable for one health care professional to use a needle or other sharp object and then leave it lying around for another to clear away. If you use it, you bin it.

There have been considerable improvements over the years in the design of containers for used sharps. The early containers, being made of cardboard, were not robust when wet and suffered from relatively frequent penetration by needles. The more recent bin designs, including plastic construction with interlocking parts and efficient sealings, have made the use of sharps bins easier and reduced the risk to porters and others transporting used equipment for disposal.

Although penetrating sharps injuries are the most common cause of transmission, other routes are important. All non-intact skin, such as abrasions and open eczematous lesions, must be covered with impervious material whenever there is the possibility of exposure to blood. This can cause difficulty, particularly for those with extensive eczematous lesions on the hands, which are inevitably made worse by prolonged use of occlusive coverings, such as surgical gloves. Most occupational physicians would recommend avoiding invasive procedures, or similar activities where there is a possibility of blood contamination, where individuals have chronic, open or moist lesions on the hands.

Protective clothing has some part to play in the prevention of occupational acquisition of HIV. The use of gloves does protect against the often minor breaks in the skin that many people have on their hands. It is often said that the wearing of gloves in procedures such as venepuncture is either not possible or causes an impairment of manual dexterity; microvascular procedures and some forms of neurosurgery give the lie to this assertion.

Personal protective equipment, such as face and eye shields, is also useful. Numerous procedures give rise to aerosolised blood which may contaminate mucous membranes of the eye or mouth. There is still some way to go in the design of protective equipment that is compatible with health care work, but plain spectacles or face shields offer a way forward in protecting the member of staff without being uncomfortable or disruptive to the procedures.

Infection control policies are the bedrock of the prevention of occupational acquisition of HIV.[6] These policies seek to minimise sharps usage and lay down standard operating procedures that are known to all. The procedures must apply across disciplines; there is no place for procedures that are owned and used by only one particular occupational group in a hospital, such as doctors or nurses.

Management of accidental exposure

Even with the best preventive measures, accidental injuries involving exposure to HIV do occur. People suffering needlestick injuries must have access to specialist occupational health advice as soon as possible after the injury. Many hospitals now run 24 hour advice lines where immediate advice on management can be given. Health care professionals naturally become extremely distressed following an accident where the transmission of HIV is a possibility; they have a right to the very best advice and support.

In managing an accidental occupational exposure, it is vital to obtain and record all available information about the accident as soon as possible. In addition to noting the date, time and place of the accident, a description of the incident should be recorded while the details are fresh in the injured person's mind. For percutaneous injuries the nature of the contaminating fluid—blood, another body fluid or concentrated virus solution—and the nature of the sharp object that pierced the skin should be recorded. If a needle or similar object is involved, the important features to record are size and whether or not the needle is hollow. Some estimate of the depth of penetration or extent of the physical injury should also be recorded.

Where the incident involved mucocutaneous contamination of the skin, the presence or otherwise of moist, open lesions, minor cuts or abrasions should be recorded, as should contamination of eyes, nose or mouth, as appropriate.

It is important to establish what is known about the HIV status of the source patient. Documentary evidence of the presence of HIV antibody should be sought; for HIV positive source patients, additional information about the CD4 count, intercurrent infections and general clinical condition is also important. In many cases of needlestick injury, when emotion is running high, it is all too easy for an oral suggestion of high risk of HIV infection in the source patient to be 'talked up' to being a proven infection. In my own experience, in more than half the cases where the source patient is alleged to be HIV positive this turns out to be untrue. There is no substitute for careful enquiry from the medical notes and laboratory reports.

Having obtained as much information as possible about the injury, it is possible to assess the risk of transmission, including the uncertainties which surround that risk estimate. Explaining this to the injured health care worker can be a time-consuming business. The evidence suggests that the most risky accidents involve percutaneous exposure to blood with a large hollow needle. Unfortunately, there are no data on which to offer precise risk estimates for each different type of accident. In discussion, the 'large hollow needle/blood' injuries should be indicated to carry a greater risk than the 0.3% 'basic risk' whilst mucocutaneous exposure to body fluids should be indicated to have a much lower risk.

Patients should initially be given an opportunity to discuss their concerns and, not infrequently, their anger. They must be reassured that the consultation will be strictly confidential.

Prophylaxis with zidovudine

It is at this stage that the question of treatment with zidovudine (AZT) will often be raised. It must be accepted that there are strong emotional pressures on the occupational physician to offer some form of treatment. This may be exacerbated where the injured health care worker is of a higher status or standing within the hospital than the occupational physician. Nevertheless, it is important that the advice and explanation given should be based on rational and logical thought.

AZT exerts its effect by providing a false substrate in viral replication. It may be said to be virostatic rather than virucidal. As such, there are no *a priori* grounds for believing that post-exposure treatment with AZT will prevent transmission. It may, in the short term, prevent viral replication but the effect of this may be simply to delay seroconversion beyond the normal time. This carries with it the at least theoretical risk that an individual may be falsely reassured that he/she has not acquired infection after the normal follow-up process.

There is no good experimental evidence that AZT does work in practice; indeed, there are a number of reports where treatment shortly after the injury has been followed by seroconversion. It must also be remembered that AZT is not licensed for this purpose; it remains a toxic therapy with uncertain long-term side effects.

Where the source patient has been treated with AZT, the virus may be heterogeneous with respect to AZT resistance. Post-exposure treatment with AZT may well select virus from the inoculate which is relatively AZT resistant. If a health care worker does become infected, future treatment with AZT may be made more difficult.

At the present time, there is no evidence to support the use, post-exposure, of AZT,[7] though such discussions with an injured health care worker may be tortuous and need to be handled with care and tact.

Testing of source patients

It is important to document the HIV status of the source patient. Most hospitals now have a routine system of testing 'identified' source patients for hepatitis B markers. Although the risks of transmission of HIV are much lower, it is increasingly the practice for the source patient to be routinely tested for HIV and, incidentally, for hepatitis C as well.

HIV testing of the source patient must not take place without consent. Experience suggests that, where consent for such testing is sought as a matter of routine by staff confident in the process, the overwhelming majority of patients readily accept. It would, of course, be wrong to apply any pressure to source patients in order to get them to accept testing; in the small number of cases where permission is withheld, the injured health care worker should be managed as if the patient were positive. This is inevitably less than satisfactory for the health care worker but the benefits of knowledge of HIV status, in terms of the management of the injury, are not sufficient to override the ethical responsibilities to the source patient.

When consent to HIV testing is being sought from the source patient, full pre-test counselling should be offered. A quick 'You don't mind, do you, Mrs Smith?' is not sufficient.

The source patient must be questioned about the possibility of his/her being infected and, in particular, a full sexual history should be taken. The implications of a positive test should be discussed, focusing on both short- and long-term implications.

The question of testing the injured health care worker should be addressed. The decision to test will depend primarily upon the wishes of the injured member of staff but will obviously be influenced by the risk assessment of the likelihood of transmission. Normal practice is to take a baseline specimen with follow-up specimens at 3 months and 6 months. Most injured health care workers are happy to be tested. Assumptions about their knowledge of HIV testing and its implications should not be made; they should have a full explanation of the test and its meaning. A common mistake when dealing with doctors is to assume a greater knowledge and thus skirt round or avoid certain issues. It can be an uncomfortable mistake for both sides.

The injury should be entered in the UK Study of Needlestick Injuries with, of course, the injured person's permission. This surveillance programme is being run by the Communicable Disease Surveillance Centre of the Public Health Laboratory Service in London, from whom further details can be obtained. It is important that as many injuries as possible be reported in order that we may redefine our risk estimates.

The injured health care worker will require advice about the 6 month follow-up period. He or she should be advised that a needlestick injury follow-up programme is not, in itself, a reason to stop undertaking exposure prone procedures. Obviously there may be particular circumstances in individual cases where this advice may be altered, for example when the risk assessment indicates a particularly high risk of infection. Nevertheless, in the overwhelming majority of cases, employment modification is not required during the follow-up period.

Health care workers should, however, be advised that they should not give blood or donate organs until the follow-up testing has demonstrated no seroconversion. It is useful to discuss the question of their future sexual activity with the advice that a barrier method of contraception would be appropriate.

It may be seen from the foregoing list of points to be covered in the management of needlestick injury that this may be better achieved in two or three consultations rather than at one sitting. If this is the case, the consultations should be close together.

It is important at this stage to ensure that the arrangements for follow-up are clearly understood and documented. Having advised the injured health care worker about the possibility of a 'seroconversion illness' between 2 and 6 weeks after exposure, it is prudent to see the injured person at about 6 weeks for a brief discussion.

The numerical risk of HIV infection after a sharps injury or other contamination incident is small. The anxiety that such injuries may provoke in health care workers is enormous and their management is both time-consuming and demanding. Nevertheless, all health care workers, in whatever setting they work, must have access to competent, specialist occupational health advice so that they receive the highest quality management of their injury.

The risk to health care professionals posed by HIV is an excellent example of the difference between hazard and risk. The virus undoubtedly presents an extreme hazard to the health and well-being of health care workers. The evidence suggests that the risk of that harm being manifest in the health care worker is comparatively low. It is the failure to appreciate the difference between hazard and risk that has made the occupational aspects of HIV so difficult to manage.

References

1. Anon (Editorial). Needlestick transmission of HTLV-III from patient infected in Africa. *Lancet* 1984; **ii**: 1376–7
2. Heptonstall J, Gill ON, Porter J, Black MB, Gilbart VL. Health care workers and HIV: surveillance of occupationally acquired infection in the UK. *Communicable Disease Report* 1993; **3**: R147–53
3. Henderson DK, Fahey BJ, Willey M, Schmitt JM, *et al.* Risk of occupational transmission of HIV-1 associated with clinical exposures. *Annals of Internal Medicine* 1990; **113**: 740–6
4. Centers for Disease Control. Update: HIV infections in health care workers exposed to the blood of infected patients. *Morbidity and Mortality Weekly Report* 1987; **36**: 285–9
5. Centers for Disease Control. Agent summary statement for HIV and report on laboratory acquired infection with HIV. *Morbidity and Mortality Weekly Report* 1988; **37**: Suppl. S4
6. Anon (Editorial). Needlesticks: preaching to the seroconverted? *Lancet* 1992; **340**: 640–2
7. Brown EM, Caul EO, Roome APCG, Glover SC, *et al.* Zidovudine after occupational exposure to HIV [letter]. *British Medical Journal* 1991; **303**: 990

2 | The viral threat: hepatitis B

Anne Cockcroft
Consultant/Senior Lecturer in Occupational Medicine, Royal Free Hampstead NHS Trust and Royal Free Hospital School of Medicine

---

Of the bloodborne viruses transmissible in the health care setting, hepatitis B poses the biggest threat to health care workers. It is also the only bloodborne virus for which there is evidence of a significant risk of infecting patients during invasive procedures and, at present, it is the only one for which an effective vaccine is available. This chapter discusses the risk of transmission of hepatitis B to health care workers and their patients, considers the mechanisms of transmission and looks at prevention of transmission by means of safe practice together with immunisation and testing of health care workers. Occupational health professionals have an important role in planning prevention programmes and in dealing with individual health care workers who have had blood exposures or who are found to be carriers of hepatitis B.

Occupational transmission of hepatitis B

Studies of infection markers

A number of surveys, mainly reflecting occupational exposures before the widespread availability of hepatitis B immunisation, have shown an increased prevalence of hepatitis B infection markers in health care workers exposed to blood and body fluids. A review[1] of evidence from a number of seroprevalence studies in the USA concluded that the overall risk to persons employed in health-related fields was four times that of the general adult population. Physicians and dentists were at five to ten times the risk of the general population, whilst groups with over ten times the risk included surgeons, clinical workers in dialysis units and mental handicap units, and laboratory workers having frequent contact with blood samples. In the UK, examination of laboratory reports of acute hepatitis B infections in the 1980s also revealed an excess rate among health care workers compared with the general population. In 1980–84 the average annual rate in men in the general population was 6 per 100,000 and up to 37 per 100,000 among health care workers.[2]

Occupations allied to health care may also carry a risk of hepatitis B infection. There is firm evidence of an increased seroprevalence of hepatitis B markers among embalmers[3] and staff in schools for mentally handicapped children,[4] but there is disagreement about the risk to emergency and public service workers. Emergency ambulance staff have been found to have an excess of hepatitis B markers[5] while ambulance staff generally,[6] police officers,[7] prison officers[8] and firemen[9] have not. Other occupations with a reported excess of hepatitis B infection include butchers,[10] hairdressers,[11] naval personnel and merchant seamen.[12]

Hazard in health care work

The most important means of transmission of hepatitis B in the health care setting is by inoculation of infected blood, either by stab

Table 1. Rate of transmission of hepatitis B after needlestick injuries from HBsAg positive source patients

	Recipients developing hepatitis B					
Author	HBeAg positive source patients		HBeAg negative source patients		All source patients	
	%	No.	%	No.	%	No.
*Seeff *et al.*[13]	22	51	1	146	6	203
†Grady *et al.*[14]	31	42	6	99	14	141
‡Werner and Grady[15]	19	234	2	156	12	390
§Hansen *et al.*[16]	—	—	—	—	3	101
#Masuko *et al.*[17]	20	56	0	43	11	99

* The recipients of HBeAg positive needlesticks shown are those who were given normal titre globulin (ISG). All hepatitis B cases among these were clinically apparent. Some of the recipients of HBeAg negative needlesticks had received HBIG.

† The recipients of needlesticks shown were those who had received ISG. Subclinical cases of hepatitis B are included.

‡ The recipients of needlesticks had received globulin of varying anti-HBs content. Subclinical cases of hepatitis B are included.

§ HBeAg status was not determined. Only clinical cases of hepatitis B were recorded and all recipients had been treated with HBIG.

Cases of subclinical hepatitis B are included. All the needlestick recipients shown were given HBIG; of 3 others with HBeAg positive needlesticks, 2 developed hepatitis B.

Source: Cockcroft A. Occupational aspects of hepatitis. In: Zuckerman AJ, Thomas HC (eds). *Viral hepatitis: scientific basis and clinical management.* London: Churchill Livingstone, 1993. pp 517–39. (Reproduced with permission.)

injuries with blood-contaminated needles (needlestick injuries) or by cuts with scalpels or other sharp instruments contaminated with blood (sharps injuries). The rate of transmission of hepatitis B after accidental inoculation of infected blood has been estimated in several studies (Table 1). Some of the studies included all cases where there was evidence of hepatitis B transmission, including asymptomatic seroconversions, while others included only clinical cases of hepatitis. These figures represent an underestimate of the transmission rate because all subjects had received some post-exposure prophylaxis, either hepatitis B immune globulin (HBIG) or normal human immunoglobulin, and an estimate for totally untreated personnel cannot be deduced. Nevertheless, Table 1 shows that the transmission risk from HBeAg positive source patients is 19–31%, while for HBeAg negative source patients it is 1–6%.

There is indirect evidence of hepatitis B transmission by non-inoculation blood contact. Hansen *et al*[16] recorded cases of clinical hepatitis B infection among employees in a medical centre; in most of the cases the employees had not reported definite exposures to blood or body fluids infected with hepatitis B. A study in a children's hospital[18] found 10 cases of hepatitis B among staff who had cared for a child with hepatitis B and a bleeding disorder but none of the 10 staff recalled needlestick injuries associated with the child although they had had frequent hand contact with his blood and did not routinely wear gloves. Hepatitis B transmission has also been reported following human bites.[19]

A study in a blood bank[20] found a high rate of hepatitis B markers among staff and presented evidence to suggest that this was due to blood contamination of minor cuts with computer test request cards. There is also evidence of an excess risk of hepatitis B infection among laboratory workers;[21] this may be related to environmental contamination with hepatitis B in laboratories.[22]

Risk to health care workers

The rate at which health care workers are exposed to hepatitis B infection depends upon the rate of accidental blood exposures and upon the prevalence of hepatitis B carriers in the patient population.

Frequency of blood exposure incidents

Blood exposure incidents are common in the health care setting, especially in operating theatres. An observational study of 1,307 surgical procedures at San Francisco General Hospital[23] revealed accidental blood exposures in 6.4% of procedures and parenteral exposure to blood in 1.7%. The risk of blood exposure was highest for procedures lasting more than 3 hours, when blood loss exceeded 300 ml, and for major vascular and gynaecological procedures. In an observational study in four hospitals in the USA, sharps injuries were noted in 6.9% of procedures,[24] and injuries were recorded by operating theatre staff in Glasgow[25] at a rate of 1.6% per surgeon per operation, calculated to give 4.6% per operation overall. Blood exposures other than sharps injuries are also common in surgical practice; these include glove tears and perforations and eye splashes with blood and other body fluids.

The risk of blood exposures is not confined to surgery. Collins and Kennedy[26] have reviewed a number of studies of sharps injuries among groups of health care workers and have reported widely varying figures (Table 2). Nurses appear to suffer the highest number of injuries both in absolute terms and when adjusted for numbers of staff employed. Other groups at risk include domestic and portering staff, who get injured from needles and other sharp instruments improperly disposed of, and laboratory staff. Relatively few injuries in the reported studies were to doctors.

Studies of reported incidents must be interpreted with caution because of the problem of under-reporting, particularly among doctors. Incident reporting rates of around 5%[27] or less[28] have been published. A recent questionnaire study of 158 operating department staff at the Royal Free Hospital in London[29] found a reporting rate of only 15% for sharps injuries.

Table 2. Incidence of needlestick injuries per 100 employee years; data from eight surveys[26]

Survey number	Nurses (all grades)	Laboratory staff	Domestics and porters
One	1.65	—	1.04
Two	13.0	10.8	16.9
Three	9.26	10.47	12.7
Four	0.86	0.62	1.71
Five	61.1	12.5	34.4
Six	23.0	18.0	12.0
Seven	9.95	6.65	10.89
Eight	2.96	—	5.4

Source: Collins CH, Kennedy DA. Microbiological hazards of occupational needlestick and 'sharps' injuries. *J Appl Microbiol* 1987; **62**:385–402.

Prevalence of hepatitis B carriers in the patient population

The Department of Health[30] have estimated the prevalence of hepatitis B carriers in the general UK adult population to be about 1 in 500, with 5–10% of these being HBeAg positive. Figures for the overall population are likely to be an underestimate of the prevalence of hepatitis B carriers in a patient population. Recent data on source patients in blood exposure incidents reported to the occupational health unit at the Royal Free Hospital in London indicate that about 3% were carriers of hepatitis B (HBsAg positive) and in one-third their hepatitis B status was not known before the incident.

Transmission from health care workers to patients

Health care workers can transmit hepatitis B infection to their patients in certain circumstances. There were 12 documented outbreaks of hepatitis B infection transmitted from infected surgical staff in the UK between 1975 and 1990, with a total of 91 infections among patients.[31] Recognised outbreaks are an underestimate of the total number of cases of hepatitis B infection acquired by patients through surgical procedures since many infections may be subclinical and the long incubation period may make tracing to a common source difficult. Notwithstanding these difficulties the UK review reported above[31] showed that the transmission rate to patients (including anicteric infections) was between 4% and 9%. A review of health care infection transmission clusters world-wide since the early 1970s[32] reported hepatitis B infection in over 300 patients and in these cases the source was usually an infected surgeon or dentist.

Gynaecological and cardiovascular surgery is particularly associated with transmission to patients[31,32] and major surgery, deep in the body cavity, carries a higher risk. In one outbreak, the transmission rate from an infected surgeon performing major obstetric or gynaecological surgery was 20% but less than 1% from the same surgeon performing medium or low risk procedures.[33] In practice the risk of transmission from health care workers to patients seems to be restricted to those workers who are HBeAg positive.[31,32]

The risk of infection transmission to patients depends upon the prevalence of infective hepatitis B carriers among populations of health care workers undertaking invasive procedures and the frequency of incidents where their blood comes into contact with the patient's circulation or open tissues. The overall prevalence of HBsAg and HBeAg among health care workers in the UK is unknown but is probably low. For example, at the Royal Free Hospital in London, among several thousand staff immunised against hepatitis B and tested for response, only two were found to be HBeAg positive; these were both laboratory workers and both were from mainland China.

The frequency of needlestick and other sharps injuries to health care workers, especially during surgical procedures, has been discussed above. One of the observational studies in the USA[24] noted that in one-third of the sharps injuries to surgical staff the needle or other sharp object recontacted the patient's tissues. On the basis of this observation it was calculated that the probability of a surgeon who is HBeAg positive transmitting to at least one patient over a 7 year period is 57–100%.[34]

Employment guidelines on hepatitis B in health care workers

In light of the continuing evidence of transmission to patients and the availability of an effective vaccine against hepatitis B, new guidelines about hepatitis B in health care workers have recently been issued by the UK Department of Health.[35] These require that health care workers performing invasive procedures must be immunised against hepatitis B *and* tested for response. Any staff who are found to be infectious carriers of the virus must not undertake exposure prone procedures, which are defined as procedures where injury to the worker may result in his or her blood contacting the patient's open tissues. Immunisation and evidence of response (or of lack of HBeAg) is a condition of employment in specialties undertaking invasive procedures and is also required for medical and dental students before they can enter their normal clinical training.

The few surgeons and dentists who are discovered to be HBeAg positive as a result of a screening programme require informed, sensitive and confidential advice. The procedures which they should not undertake should be agreed locally between the health care worker and other professionals such as virologists, infection control specialists and occupational physicians. In difficult cases advice is available from a UK expert panel. Restrictions of practice may sometimes be temporary since some individuals become HBeAg negative either with time or as a result of treatment. The question of compensation may also arise and in the UK hepatitis B is a prescribed industrial disease for health care workers.

Health care employers need to develop policies for the management of employees with hepatitis B infection, which cover medical, ethical and practical issues.[36] The Department of Health guidelines recommend that a specialist occupational physician should be involved in developing policies and in dealing with individual health care workers infected with hepatitis B. It is important to recognise the concerns which health care workers may have about compulsory screening; not the least of these is the fear that HIV screening may be next. The new guidelines can only be implemented successfully with the full cooperation of the clinical staff concerned.

Prevention of occupational transmission

It should be possible to eliminate occupational transmission almost entirely by vaccination of health care workers against hepatitis B, with testing of response. However, coverage with immunisation programmes is usually incomplete and some people fail to respond to vaccine. It is also important not to give the impression that, once immunised against hepatitis B, staff can be exposed to blood with impunity. Programmes to prevent occupational transmission of hepatitis B and other bloodborne viruses should include safe practices to reduce hazardous exposures and proper management of blood exposure incidents.

Safe working practices

There are two general approaches to safe practice with regard to prevention of transmission of bloodborne infections: the 'traditional' infection control approach and the more recent universal precautions approach. In the traditional approach, patients or specimens known or suspected to be infected are identified and special precautions are taken in their care or processing. The universal precautions approach is based on the premise that the blood of all patients should be treated as potentially infectious; the level of precautions to be taken should depend upon a risk assessment of the procedures being undertaken rather than of the patient's infection status.

The arguments for the two approaches in relation to HIV infection have been rehearsed recently.[37] In favour of the traditional approach it is argued that the provision of a high level of protection in all cases is expensive and not justifiable and that therefore control measures should be applied for selected cases. However, identification of patients infected with HIV or hepatitis B on the basis of history is not reliable[38] and routine screening of patients would be expensive without providing any direct protection to staff. Furthermore, awaiting test results is not feasible in emergency situations, where exposure to blood is frequent, and importantly, knowledge of patients' 'high risk' status does not seem to reduce the risk of blood exposures during surgical procedures.[24]

Despite the simplicity and logic of universal precautions, health care workers do not always practise them even when it is official policy to do so.[39] A majority of clinical medical students and consultants at a London hospital reported changing their clinical practice—mainly by wearing gloves and by taking care with needles—if they knew a patient was infected with a bloodborne virus.[40]

Preventing inoculation injuries is of prime importance. In surgery this can be helped by using instruments to handle needles during suturing, alternative wound closure techniques (such as stapling), the use of blunt needles for suturing adipose tissue and avoidance of the use of sharp instruments where possible. Providing and maintaining effective systems for the collection and disposal of used sharp instruments is also critical.[41]

Hepatitis B immunisation programmes

A safe, effective vaccine against hepatitis B has been licensed in the UK for more than a decade. The Department of Health Joint Committee on Vaccination and Immunisation[42] recommends hepatitis B immunisation for all health care workers at risk of exposure to blood likely to be infected with hepatitis B. Furthermore, immunisation, with testing of response, is now required for all health care workers involved in exposure prone procedures.[35] Very high rates of seroconversion (95% and above) following hepatitis B immunisation given into the deltoid muscle can be achieved among health care workers.[43]

Employers have a responsibility to protect workers against occupational hazards; in the UK hepatitis B, as a biological hazard, is covered by the Control of Substances Hazardous to Health (COSHH) Regulations 1988. Provision of immunisation would appear to be a key component of the control measures required under the regulations. Despite this, a survey of hospital occupational health departments in 1988 revealed that many of their programmes of hepatitis B immunisation for staff were limited by the cost of the vaccine and the resources of the departments.[44]

Even when immunisation programmes are available, not all health care workers participate. A number of recent studies have found incomplete hepatitis B immunisation among groups of health care workers (Table 3). Reported reasons for the low uptake rates include apathy, lack of knowledge about vaccine efficacy, fears about vaccine safety and lack of knowledge about hepatitis B transmission. Among surgeons, prior to the new guidelines,[35] there has also been a fear that being a non-responder may lead to career problems.

Workers occupationally exposed to hepatitis B should be tested for response after immunisation; this is now a requirement for those involved in invasive procedures, in order to confirm that they are not infectious carriers of hepatitis B. A scheme for post-immunisation testing is shown in Fig 1. Individuals with a low antibody response (anti-HBs <100 IU/l) or no antibody response (anti-HBs <10 IU/l) are tested further for evidence of previous infection. Low and non-responders without anti-HBc ('simple non-responders') can be offered further doses of vaccine. Individuals with both anti-HBs and anti-HBc can be reassured that they are immune due to previous infection but are not carriers of hepatitis B. Those with anti-HBc and without anti-HBs could be carriers; they need to be counselled and tested for HBsAg. If they are positive for HBsAg, they need to be tested for HBeAg and anti-HBe to establish their infectivity status. Workers who are HBsAg positive but HBeAg negative can be allowed to continue exposure prone procedures, unless there is evidence that they have transmitted hepatitis B to patients.[35]

Persistent non-responders (with no evidence of previous infection) need to be made aware that they are not protected against hepatitis B. They need to understand the importance of safe practice and immediate reporting of blood exposure incidents so that post-exposure prophylaxis can be given if necessary. It may be possible for non-responders to avoid certain duties; for example, porters who do not respond should not collect sharps boxes. Some

1. Test for anti-HBs 1–3 months after third dose of vaccine.
2. Test for anti-HBc in all with low (< 100 IU/l) or absent (< 10 IU/l) anti-HBs response.
3. If no anti-HBc = simple non-responder.
4. If anti-HBc present = evidence of previous infection.
    - with anti-HBs: no further action
    - without anti-HBs: further tests required.
5. Test for HBsAg in those with anti-HBc and no anti-HBs. If HBsAg positive, test for HBeAg and anti-HBe.

Fig 1. *Scheme for hepatitis B post-immunisation antibody testing*

Table 3. Hepatitis B immunisation rates among groups of health care workers

Authors	Occupational group	Number studied	% immunised	% antibody checked*
Berridge *et al.*[45]	Vascular surgeons	206	64	45
Williams and Flowerdew[46]	General surgeons	76	87	47
Porteous[47]	Orthopaedic surgeons	800	69	—
Williams *et al.*[29]	Operating theatre staff	158	78	81
Astbury and Baxter[27]	Hospital staff	803	25	—
Spence and Dash[48]	Nurses in 'high risk' areas	169	42	—
Wood[49]	GP principals	416	35	—
	Trainees	32	69	—
Van Damme *et al.*[50]	Belgian GPs	149	44	—
	Dentists	126	71	—
Choudhury and Cleator[51]	Clinical medical students	172	95	83
Newman and Hambling[52]	Hospital staff in blood exposures	2,975	49	Checked at time of incident
Oakley *et al.*[53]	Hospital staff in blood exposures	438	71	Checked at time of incident

* Percentage of those immunised who had anti-HBs response measured.

Source: Cockcroft A. Occupational aspects of hepatitis. In: Zuckerman AJ, Thomas HC (eds). *Viral hepatitis: scientific basis and clinical management.* London: Churchill Livingstone, 1993. (Reproduced with permission.)

people believe that non-responders undertaking invasive procedures should be tested for HBsAg at intervals to ensure that they have not become carriers, but this is not a requirement of the Department of Health guidelines.[35]

For people with a continuing occupational risk of hepatitis B infection, maintaining adequate levels of protection after immunisation seems important. There is still debate about whether booster doses of vaccine are needed, and at what intervals, following an initial adequate response. Many would argue that a booster dose at about 5 years is appropriate, although it is clear that there is considerable inter-individual variation in the rate of decay of antibody levels.

Management of blood exposure incidents

Proper management of blood exposure incidents can reduce the risk of hepatitis B transmission, even if the worker involved has not been previously immunised against hepatitis B. Management should include establishing the worker's hepatitis B immune status, testing known source patients for HBsAg (and HBeAg) and administering HBIG and hepatitis B vaccine if necessary. A protocol for the management of blood exposure incidents with regard to hepatitis B is described in recent guidance from the Communicable Disease Surveillance Centre.[54] For non-vaccinated workers, the use of HBIG is recommended, together with the first dose of vaccine, if the source patient is known to be HBsAg positive. For vaccine non-responders, the use of HBIG may sometimes be appropriate, even when the source patient is unknown, if there is a significant risk of their being HBsAg positive (eg from an area with a high proportion of patients with hepatitis B infection). For people who have previously responded to vaccine, a booster dose of vaccine is sufficient and HBIG is not indicated even if the source is HBsAg positive. Post-exposure active immunisation following any incident is important for the future protection of unvaccinated staff, since those reporting incidents are clearly at risk.

HBIG alone is clearly not completely effective; for example, in one study 20% of staff who had sustained needlestick injuries from HBeAg positive source patients developed hepatitis B, despite receiving HBIG within 48 hours.[17] As the protection conferred by post-exposure prophylaxis in non-immune individuals is likely to be incomplete, it is important that they be followed up, especially if the source patient is HBeAg positive.

Management of blood exposure incidents should be undertaken

by a specified department, ideally the occupational health department where there is one available, and the arrangements for reporting incidents should be widely publicised among all employees. The management of incidents should be regularly reviewed so that problems can be identified and dealt with.

Summary

Hepatitis B is a serious occupational risk but one that is potentially preventable. Occupational physicians have a key role both in ensuring that suitable policies are implemented and in dealing with individual members of staff exposed to infection or who are carriers of the virus.

References

1. West DJ. The risk of hepatitis B infection among health professionals in the United States: a review. *American Journal of the Medical Sciences* 1985; **287**: 26–33
2. Struve J, Aronsson B, Frenning B, Forsgren M, Weiland O. Prevalence of hepatitis B virus markers and exposure to occupational risks likely to be associated with acquisition of hepatitis B virus among health care workers in Stockholm. *Journal of Infection* 1992; **24**: 147–56
3. Turner SB, Kunches LM, Gordon KF, Travers PH, Mueller NE. Public health briefs. Occupational exposure to human immunodeficiency virus (HIV) and hepatitis B virus among embalmers: a pilot seroprevalence study. *American Journal of Public Health* 1989; **79**: 1425–6
4. Remis RS, Rossignol MA, Kane MA. Hepatitis B infection in a day school for mentally retarded students: transmission from students to staff. *American Journal of Public Health* 1987; **77**: 1183–6
5. Kunches LM, Craven DE, Werner BG, Jacobs LM. Hepatitis B exposure in emergency medical personnel: prevalence of serologic markers and need for immunization. *American Journal of Medicine* 1983; **75**: 269–72
6. Morgan-Capner P, Wallice PDB. Hepatitis B markers in ambulance personnel in Lancashire. *Journal of the Society of Occupational Medicine* 1990; **40**: 21–2
7. Peterkin M, Crawford RJ. Hepatitis B vaccine for police forces? *Lancet* 1986; **ii**: 1458–9
8. Radvan GH, Hewson EG, Berenger S, Brookman DJ. The Newcastle hepatitis B outbreak: observations on cause, management, and prevention. *Medical Journal of Australia* 1986; **144**: 461–4
9. Crosse BA, Teale C, Lees EM. Hepatitis B markers in West Yorkshire firemen. *Epidemiology and Infection* 1989; **103**: 383–5
10. Gerlich WH, Thomssen R. Outbreak of hepatitis B at a butcher's shop. *Deutsch Medizin Wochenschrift* 1982; **107**: 1627–30

11. Watt AD. Hairdressers and hepatitis B: a risk of inapparent parenteral infection. *Journal of the Society of Occupational Medicine* 1987; **37**: 124–5
12. Hyams KC, Palinkas LA, Burr RG. Viral hepatitis in the US navy, 1975–1984. *American Journal of Epidemiology* 1989; **130**: 319–26
13. Seeff LB, Wright EC, Zimmerman HJ, *et al.* Type B hepatitis after needlestick exposure: prevention with hepatitis immune globulin. Final report of the Veterans Administration Cooperative Study. *Annals of Internal Medicine* 1978; **88**: 285–93
14. Grady GF, Lee VA, Prince AM, *et al.* Hepatitis B immune globulin for accidental exposures among medical personnel: final report of a multicenter controlled trial. *Journal of Infectious Diseases* 1978; **138**: 625–38
15. Werner BA, Grady GF. Accidental hepatitis B surface antigen positive inoculations. *Annals of Internal Medicine* 1982; **97**: 367–9
16. Hansen JP, Falconer JA, Hamilton JD, Herpok FJ. Hepatitis B in a medical center. *Journal of Occupational Medicine* 1981; **23**: 338–42
17. Masuko K, Mitsui T, Iwano K, *et al.* Factors influencing postexposure immunoprophylaxis of hepatitis B virus infection with hepatitis B immune globulin. *Gastroenterology* 1985; **88**: 151–5
18. Bryan JA, Carr HE, Gregg MB. An outbreak of nonparenterally transmitted hepatitis B. *Journal of the American Medical Association* 1973; **223**: 279–83
19. MacQuarrie MB, Forghani B, Wolochow DA. Hepatitis B transmitted by a human bite. *Journal of the American Medical Association* 1974; **230**: 723–4
20. Pattison CP, Boyer KM, Maynard JE, Kelly PC. Epidemic hepatitis in a clinical laboratory: possible association with computer card handling. *Journal of the American Medical Association* 1974; **230**: 854–7
21. Anderson RA, Woodfield DG. Hepatitis B virus infections in laboratory staff. *New Zealand Medical Journal* 1982; **95**: 69–71
22. Evans MR, Henderson DK, Bennett JE. Potential for laboratory exposures to biohazardous agents found in blood. *American Journal of Public Health* 1990; **80**: 423–7
23. Gerberding JL, Littell C, Tarkington A, Brown A, Schecter WP. Risk of exposure of surgical personnel to patients' blood during surgery at San Francisco General Hospital. *New England Journal of Medicine* 1990; **322**: 1788–93
24. Tokars J, Bell D, Marcus R, *et al.* Percutaneous injuries during surgical procedures. *Proceedings of the VII International Conference on AIDS,* 1991; Vol 2, Florence, Italy, p 83
25. Camilleri AE, Murray S, Imrie CW. Needlestick injuries in surgeons: what is the incidence? *Journal of the Royal College of Surgeons of Edinburgh* 1991; **36**: 317–8
26. Collins CH, Kennedy DA. Microbiological hazards of occupational needlestick and 'sharps' injuries. *Journal of Applied Microbiology* 1987; **62**: 385–402
27. Astbury C, Baxter PJ. Infection risks in hospital staff from blood: hazardous injury rates and acceptance of hepatitis B immunization. *Journal of the Society of Occupational Medicine* 1990; **40**: 92–3
28. McGeer A, Sinor AE, Low DE. Epidemiology of needlestick injuries in house officers. *Journal of Infectious Diseases* 1990; **162**: 961–4

29. Williams S, Gooch C, Cockcroft A. Hepatitis B immunisation and blood exposure incidents amongst operating department staff. *British Journal of Surgery* 1993; **80**: 714–6
30. Department of Health. *Guidance for clinical health care workers: protection against infection with HIV and hepatitis viruses*. London: HMSO, 1990
31. Heptonstall J. Outbreaks of hepatitis B virus infection associated with infected surgical staff. *Communicable Disease Report* 1991; **1**: R81–5
32. Centers for Disease Control. Recommendations for preventing transmission of human immunodeficiency virus and hepatitis B virus to patients during exposure-prone procedures. *Morbidity and Mortality Weekly Report* 1991; **40**: 2–3
33. Welch J, Webster M, Tilzey AJ, Noah ND, Banatvala JE. Hepatitis B infections after gynaecological surgery. *Lancet* 1989; **i**: 205–7
34. Bell DM, Martone WJ, Cuiver DH, *et al.* Risk of endemic HIV and hepatitis B virus (HBV) transmission to patients during invasive procedures. *Proceedings of the Seventh International Conference on AIDS*. Florence, 1991, p 37
35. Department of Health. *Protecting health care workers and their patients from hepatitis B*. London: Department of Health, 1993
36. Williams S, Cockcroft A. Policies for HIV and hepatitis B infected health care workers. *Occupational Health Review* 1992; **36**: 12–14
37. Shanson DC, Cockcroft A. Forum: Testing patients for HIV antibodies is useful for infection control purposes. *Reviews in Medical Virology* 1991; **1**: 5–9
38. Parry CM, Harries AD, Beeching NJ, Rothburn MM. Phlebotomy in inoculation risk patients: a questionnaire survey of knowledge and practices of hospital doctors in Liverpool. *Journal of Hospital Infections* 1991; **18**: 313–8
39. Kelen GD, DiGiovanni TA, Celentano DD, *et al.* Adherence to universal (barrier) precautions during interventions on critically ill and injured emergency department patients. *Journal of AIDS* 1990; **3**: 987–94
40. Elford J, Cockcroft A. Compulsory HIV antibody testing, universal precautions and the perceived risk of HIV: a survey among medical students and consultant staff at a London teaching hospital. *AIDS Care* 1991; **3**: 151–8
41. British Medical Association. *A code of practice for the safe use and disposal of sharps*. London: BMA, 1990
42. Department of Health, Joint Committee on Vaccination and Immunisation. *Immunisation against infectious disease*. London: HMSO, 1990
43. Cockcroft A, Soper P, Insall C, *et al.* Antibody response following hepatitis B immunization in a group of health care workers. *British Journal of Industrial Medicine* 1990; **47**: 199–202
44. Baddick MR, Aw T-C. Immunisation against hepatitis B among NHS staff in West Midlands Regional Health Authority. *British Medical Journal* 1989; **299**: 607
45. Berridge DC, Galea MH, Evans DF, Pugh S, *et al.* Hepatitis B immunisation in vascular surgeons. *British Journal of Surgery* 1990; **77**: 585–6
46. Williams JR, Flowerdew ADS. Uptake of immunisation against

hepatitis B among surgeons in Wessex Regional Health Authority. *British Medical Journal* 1990; **301**: 154

47. Porteous MJLeF. Operating practices of and precautions taken by orthopaedic surgeons to avoid infection with HIV and hepatitis B virus during surgery. *British Medical Journal* 1990; **301**: 167–9
48. Spence MR, Dash GP. Hepatitis B: perceptions, knowledge and vaccine acceptance among registered nurses in high-risk occupations in a university hospital. *Infection Control and Hospital Epidemiology* 1990; **11**: 129–33
49. Wood A. Hepatitis B vaccination and GPs. *Practitioner* 1989; **233**: 1067–8.
50. Van Damme P, de Cock G, Cramm M, Eylenbosch W. Precautions taken by orthopaedic surgeons to avoid infection with HIV and hepatitis B virus [letter]. *British Medical Journal* 1990; **301**: 611
51. Choudhury RP, Cleator SJ. An examination of needlestick injury rates, hepatitis B vaccination uptake and instruction on 'sharps' technique among medical students. *Journal of Hospital Infection* 1992; **22**: 143–8
52. Newman CPS, Hambling MH. Hazardous incidents and immunity to hepatitis B. *Communicable Disease Report* 1992; **2**: R30–1
53. Oakley K, Gooch C, Cockcroft A. Review of management of incidents involving exposure to blood in a London teaching hospital, 1989–91. *British Medical Journal* 1992; **304**: 949–51
54. PHLS Hepatitis Subcommittee. Exposure to hepatitis B virus: guidance on post-exposure prophylaxis. *Communicable Disease Report* 1992; **2**: R97–101

3 | Hepatitis C

Geoffrey M Dusheiko
Royal Free Hospital and School of Medicine, London

The discovery of hepatitis C in 1989 and the development of serological and nucleic acid diagnostic tests indicated the prevalence and importance of this disease. Current diagnostic markers now enable the prevalence and transmission of hepatitis C in health care settings to be estimated.

The complete nucleotide sequence of the HCV genome has been determined in a number of isolates. The virus is a positive strand RNA virus of approximately 9,400 nucleotides and consists of one long open reading frame encoding a polyprotein of 3,010–3,033 amino acids which is cleaved into functionally distinct polypeptides during or after translation. Its organisation is similar to that of pestiviruses and flaviviruses of the family Flaviviridae but it is classified within its own genus. The nucleocapsid and envelope proteins are encoded at the 5' end of the genome and the non-structural elements are located at the 3' region.

The total or partial nucleotide sequences obtained from a number of isolates indicate that HCV may be divided into several major types (thus far six, or possibly nine) with component subtypes based upon nucleotide homology.[1–4] There are hypervariable regions of the genome, especially in the E1 and E2 domains. These putative envelope regions may be important antigenic sites and their variability may be critical to persistence of infection and immunopathogenesis.

At least 50% of persons infected with HCV develop chronic infection; there is a spectrum of disease in those chronically infected. The disease has a long natural history and may be benign and asymptomatic for several decades, but severe disease, including cirrhosis, hepatic decompensation and hepatocellular failure, may ensue in a proportion.

Transmission and epidemiology

Infection with hepatitis C is seen most clearly after transfusion of whole-blood products, but in many countries it has been acquired by community transmission. In some regions, for example southern Europe, Africa (eg Egypt and Cameroon) and Japan, the prevalence of hepatitis C is relatively high and 1.5–10% of the general population have evidence of infection.

Serological testing has shown a high prevalence of anti-HCV in patients with chronic active hepatitis and/or cirrhosis considered to be due to non-A,non-B (NANB) hepatitis.[5] There is a high prevalence of hepatitis C in haemophiliacs, thalassaemics, haemodialysed patients, transplant recipients, intravenous drug abusers and, in some countries, dentists.[6] Intrafamilial and intraspousal transmission may occur but appears to be relatively infrequent in developed countries. Maternal infant transmission has been documented in mothers with higher levels of viraemia, and human immunodeficiency virus (HIV) coinfection, but this also appears to be infrequent.[7,8]

Clinical and laboratory features

Acute hepatitis C

The mean incubation period of hepatitis C is 6–12 weeks. However, with large inocula, such as following administration of factor VIII, the period is reduced.[9,10] The acute course of HCV infection is clinically mild, and the peak serum alanine aminotransferase (ALT) elevations are less than those encountered in acute hepatitis A or B. Only 25% of cases are icteric. HCV frequently causes acute disease that is asymptomatic and unnoticed. During the early clinical phase the serum ALT levels may fluctuate, and may become normal or near normal, making the determination of true convalescence difficult.

The average time from transfusion to seroconversion with the second generation tests is of the order of 7–8 weeks; anti-c33 or anti-c22 not infrequently appear a week or two earlier than anti-c100-3. Seroconversion occurs much less frequently, and in lower titre, in acute self-limiting infections than in those that progress to become chronic.[5,11] Serological testing now indicates that seroconversion to anti-HCV occurs in 85–100% of patients with chronic post-transfusion NANB hepatitis.[12] A proportion of patients with post-transfusion and sporadically acquired NANB hepatitis remain anti-HCV seronegative; it will be important to define whether these patients represent HCV infection with poor serological response or due to other unclassified NANB agents.

The acute disease may resolve completely with clearance of HCV

RNA from serum. There is no suitable immunodiagnostic test for resolved infection and immunity. The acute disease may resolve in 25–50% of cases but it is well known that it becomes chronic in more than half. In some patients a very early appearance of anti-HCV may be due to passively acquired antibody from donor blood.

Serum HCV RNA has been detected by polymerase chain reaction (PCR) testing within 1–3 weeks of transfusion in patients with hepatitis C; it usually lasts less than 4 months in patients with acute self-limited hepatitis C but may persist for decades in patients with chronic disease.[13,14]

Chronic hepatitis C

Most cases of chronic hepatitis C are not preceded by an episode of clinically apparent, icteric hepatitis. Fifty to seventy-five per cent of patients with type C post-transfusion or sporadic hepatitis continue to have abnormal serum aminotransferase levels after 12 months, and chronic hepatitis histologically.[15] Serum aminotransferases decline from the peak values encountered in the acute phase of the disease, but typically remain 2–8-fold abnormal. Serum ALT concentrations may fluctuate over time, and may even intermittently be normal.

Many patients have a sustained elevation of the serum aminotransferases. The natural history of the disease is variable; anti-HCV persists for years and even decades in chronic hepatitis C but may decline in titre or disappear with resolution. Antibodies to envelope proteins are found in 95% of patients with chronic infection. A small percentage of patients appear to eradicate HCV RNA permanently after chronic infection but it is usually less than 5–10%.[5,16]

HCV RNA usually persists in patients with abnormal serum aminotransferases and anti-HCV. Although most patients with raised serum ALT are HCV RNA positive, conversely HCV RNA may be detectable in patients with normal serum ALT. Isolates of HCV in individual patients may show nucleotide substitutions with time, suggesting that the HCV RNA mutates at a rate similar to that of other RNA viruses.[17] The emergence of a mutant population does not always correlate with peaks in ALT.

It is not easy to project the prognosis for patients seen at one point in time. Episodes of hepatic necrosis may progress at variable rates to cirrhosis but in some patients the lesion may revert to inactive hepatitis. Cirrhosis may develop in patients with initial mild histological pattern; the mechanism for this transition is not known but it may occur after repeated attacks of lobular necrosis associated with piecemeal necrosis. However, a relationship between histological exacerbations and episodic clinical course is not proven. The morphological features of cirrhosis due to hepatitis C are not specific to the disease; in the earlier stages, lymphoid aggregates may be seen.

It is believed that 10–20% of patients with chronic hepatitis C infections will progress to cirrhosis within a decade, albeit cirrhosis that remains indolent and only slowly progressive for a prolonged period.[14,18–20] The disease is not necessarily benign, however, and rapidly progressive cirrhosis can occur. Typically patients have an indolent disease, and the onset of cirrhosis is slow, only developing after age 20–30 and in a minority of patients. The risk of further progression is probably cumulative but is influenced by other cofactors which may include viral genotype, level of viraemia, other viral infection, immunosuppression and age of acquisition. Older age at infection, concomitant alcohol abuse and concurrent HBV or HIV infection or other illness may be important aggravating cofactors. In those with progressive infection, persistent infection may lead progressively to chronic active hepatitis, cirrhosis, portal hypertension and hepatocellular carcinoma (HCC).

Older patients may present with complications of cirrhosis, or even HCC. With progressive disease the laboratory values become progressively more abnormal. The finding of aspartate aminotransferase (AST) greater than ALT, low albumin and prolonged prothrombin time suggest cirrhosis, and low levels of autoantibodies may become detectable. The infection also causes systemic disease and may be associated with a number of systemic complications including a form of autoimmune hepatitis, cryoglobulinaemia,[21] membranous glomerulonephritis, porphyria cutanea tarda, lymphocytic sialadenitis and lichen planus. Lymphoma has been reported in patients with chronic hepatitis C.

Hepatitis C and health care professions

Centers for Disease Control surveillance data in the USA have indicated that in 5% of patients the only source of HCV infection is occupational exposure. It can be assumed that HCV is present in several body fluids of infected patients, particularly in blood, and hepatitis C is known to replicate in peripheral blood mononuclear cells.[22] Saliva may also contain infectious HCV particles, and may transmit hepatitis C.[23]

Although the overall risk of acquisition of hepatitis C in

Table 1. Risk of hepatitis C in health care workers (data from Ref 26)

Group	Total	Number positive
Local blood donors: anti-HBc positive	104,239	1,879 (1.8%)
Hospital personnel: anti-HBc positive	943	59 (6.2%)
Hospital personnel: anti-HCV positive	943	7 (0.7%)
Blood donors: anti-HCV positive	104,239	416 (0.4%)

hospitals is low, transmission may occur[24] (Table 1). This was first suggested after NANB hepatitis was transmitted to chimpanzees by intravenous inoculation of a human serum sample obtained from a patient with the clinical and serological diagnosis of chronic NANB hepatitis. The patient's blood had earlier been shown to transmit the disease to a nurse, after an accidental needlestick. Neither the nurse nor the original patient had serological evidence of infection with hepatitis A, hepatitis B, cytomegalovirus or Epstein–Barr virus.[25] Now, with an assay to detect HCV infection, it has become easier to verify transmission of type C hepatitis from patients to health care workers, and several clinical case reports have substantiated that transmission can occur.

The prevalence of hepatitis B and C viral hepatitis in health care personnel has been determined in several studies.[26,27] This risk is lower than that observed in, for example, intravenous drug abusers (70.8%), patients with HIV virus (11.6%), prostitutes (8.8%) and even volunteer blood donors (0.5–1.4%), but certain studies have indicated a higher risk of hepatitis C to practitioners in some health care sectors and in some countries; in New York the prevalence was 1.7% in dentists and 9.3% in oral surgeons.[28]

In a study of patients attending an emergency department, 18.2% were anti-HCV positive; thus emergency surgery or invasive procedures in this setting may constitute a particular risk to nursing, medical and paramedical personnel. Possible mechanisms of transmission include stab injuries or needlestick episodes. The risk of the recipient of an anti-HCV positive needlestick developing hepatitis C is considered to be low compared with that for recipients of anti-HCV positive blood transfusions and the 60% risk of hepatitis B after a needlestick from an HBeAg positive patient. Thus the majority of anti-HCV positive patients will not transmit hepatitis C via a needlestick; this appears to be due to the fact that HCV circulates at relatively low titres in human sera, and the infecting titre from most patients with hepatitis C is lower than that occurring in HBsAg and HBeAg positive sera.

This low risk (0–3%) of needlestick injuries in transmission of HCV in hospital personnel has been suggested by several studies.[29] A study in Barcelona followed employees for 12 months after parenteral exposure to an anti-HCV source. None developed hepatitis, and moreover none seroconverted to anti-HCV (by ELISA II) after this time.[30]

However, several large studies elsewhere have found higher rates of transmission (up to 10%) after needlesticks. Two studies have been reported in Japanese hospital personnel. Mitsui *et al.* followed cases of needlestick exposure that did not involve HBsAg positive patients.[31] Sixty-eight index cases were from needlestick exposure to anti-HCV positive (ELISA II) and HCV RNA positive patients. Seven medical personnel were infected with hepatitis C after the accident. The hepatitis that occurred in these cases was generally subclinical or self-limiting, but one of the seven did have persistent aminotransferase elevations. Thus in this study the risk of transmission was 10%.

A second Japanese study documented the outcome in 196 anti-HCV negative persons after 200 needlestick exposures at Shinshu University Hospital. One hundred and seven of these (53%) involved anti-HCV positive donors. Four of 110 (4%) of the recipients of an anti-HCV positive needlestick developed hepatitis; in only three was hepatitis accompanied by seroconversion to anti-HCV. Two recipients had abnormal serum ALT at 12 months.[32]

In a fourth study, acute hepatitis was reported in 3.3% of hospital personnel after needlestick accidents involving anti-HCV positive patients.[33] There are also individual case reports of transmission of hepatitis C by needlestick exposure.[34]

Thus, although transmission is infrequent, it does occur and chronic hepatitis may ensue. Although the incidence of hepatitis following needlestick exposure to an HCV positive patient is not as high as following exposure to hepatitis B, it is probably higher than that after exposure to HIV positive blood (0.5%). A case report has documented transmission to a surgeon with needlestick exposure to an HIV positive intravenous drug abuser; the surgeon developed acute hepatitis and seroconversion to anti-HCV.[35] Other potential sources of exposure to workers in a hospital setting include contamination via blood splash into the conjunctiva[36] and via a human bite.[37]

Factors that might influence the risk of transmission include the size of inoculum, the infecting dose, the level of viraemia and the presence of immune complexes of HCV antigens and antibodies. The cotransmission of hepatitis B, C and HIV[38] suggests that trans-

Table 2. Hepatitis C and HIV transmission: risk to female partners of HIV and/or HCV infected haemophiliac men (data from Ref 38)

Status in men	Status in women	
	HCV infection	HIV infection
HIV + HCV positive	5/164 (3%)	21/164 (13%)
HCV alone	0/30	—
HIV positive/HCV indeterminate	—	4/32 (13%)

mission of hepatitis B is more efficient. In studies of HIV/HCV coinfection the frequency of HCV transmission to sexual partners is five times higher when HIV is also transmitted. This influence has been demonstrated in sexual partners of coinfected haemophiliac men. When a single virus has been transmitted to the female sexual partner, this is more often HIV than HCV[38] (Table 2).

Nosocomial transmission

Potential nosocomial sources of transmission of hepatitis C include autolet guards,[39] spring loaded lancet devices[40] or multiple use heparin vials, as has been reported for hepatitis B, but clusters of cases due to these devices have not been reported. There are several case reports of nosocomial or health care associated transmission of hepatitis C, including haemodialysis patient to nurse transmission; this has occurred even when the donor was PCR positive but anti-HCV negative.[41]

HCV transmission by tattooing needle has been documented.[42] Other routes include skin vacuum therapy, called 'Sui dama' therapy in Japan, which has been associated with a cluster of cases in that country.

Type C hepatitis is relatively common amongst haemodialysis patients, and staff in these units are at risk because of the multiple needle punctures often required in the patients. The prevalence of hepatitis C in dialysed patients varies in different geographic regions, reflecting the background prevalence of hepatitis C in the blood donor population and health care control measures. Clustering of cases may occur in high risk areas. For example, in 1988, 45% of 77 patients undergoing chronic haemodialysis developed an ALT increase and anti-HCV was later found in 82% of probable cases. The outbreak was ascribed to inadequate infection control

Table 3. Hospitalised patients with higher rates of hepatitis C and of transmission

- Haemophiliacs
- Intravenous drug users
- Recipients of whole blood, transfusable components: lymphoma, leukaemia
- Thalassaemics
- Liver transplant recipients
- Patients with cirrhosis, chronic hepatitis or liver cancer
- Renal dialysis patients
- Renal transplant recipients
- Bone marrow transplant recipients
- Patients with HIV infection
- Homosexual men(?)
- Patients in rheumatology clinics
- Sexually transmitted disease clinic referrals
- Organ donors

procedures and breaks in infection control in the unit, but none of the staff was anti-HCV positive.[43]

Patients with higher rates of hepatitis C and of transmission are shown in Table 3.[44,45] Since hepatitis C is so often a 'silent' or asymptomatic infection, universal precautions should be taken when handling blood samples from all patients. Moreover, the identification of patients with hepatitis C should not lead to discrimination or have a negative impact on their care. The pre-operative testing and legality of testing has not been addressed, but the same principles apply as in treating patients with hepatitis B and HIV infection.

Transmission from health care workers to patients

There are two anecdotal, preliminary reports of transmission of hepatitis C from a surgeon to patients: a case report from Spain (Barcelona) and possibly one in the United Kingdom. These cases have been verified by molecular epidemiological evidence, using PCR typing to compare nucleotide sequence homology in corresponding patients, as has been done with familial or maternal infant transmission.[46,47] The circumstances of these transmissions are not yet established, and it is unknown whether higher levels of viraemia and particular forms of surgery are more likely to transmit infection.

In the absence of detailed information, advisory groups for hepatitis in the UK and the USA have decided that surgeons or obstetricians (and presumably venesectionists and nurses) should be allowed to continue unrestricted practice unless they have been shown to transmit infection to a patient. Surgeons should be informed that antiviral therapy is effective in a proportion of patients with hepatitis C.

The question of surgical transmission by surgeons is likely to remain a vexing ethical and legal issue. The rationale for allowing surgeons to continue operating can be questioned. Should we wait for outbreaks of hepatitis C to be identified before deciding on the wisdom of allowing surgeons infected with HCV to continue unrestricted practice? Is advice on double gloving for infected surgeons enough? As there are already reports of transmission, it is likely that more will emerge as awareness increases. Surgeons will be aware that these guidelines are not likely to prevent litigation if, despite knowing that they are anti-HCV and HCV RNA positive, they continue operating and are implicated in transmission of hepatitis C.

Prevention

Appropriate precautions to protect health care workers are needed, and every effort to avoid careless accidental exposure should be made. The risk of chronic infection is high, and there are questions regarding the effectiveness of host immunity to HCV. Guidelines have been published by the Surgical Infection Society for working procedures in the operating room,[48] but there is less information regarding the sterilisation and inactivation of equipment.

Post-exposure prophylaxis still poses a problem. Although it is possible that immune serum globulin may decrease the incidence of post-transfusion NANB hepatitis, this has not been conclusively demonstrated for hepatitis C needlestick exposures. Although the efficacy of prophylactic polyvalent immunoglobulin is unknown, its use has been recommended by the Immunization Advisory Committee in the USA.[29]

The value of interferon-alpha given as post-exposure prophylaxis is unknown. If hepatitis develops, interferon-alpha given during the acute phase of hepatitis may decrease the risk of chronic hepatitis, but this may require a year of treatment.

General measures and universal precautions will reduce the risk of transmission. Such guidelines have been published for hepatitis

B;[49] similar good work practices, with appropriate equipment and strategies, apply.

Exposure incidents will benefit from a comprehensive plan, including counselling.[50] As hepatitis C often causes subclinical infection, needlestick recipients will need follow-up, measuring serum aminotransferases and anti-HCV, and possibly HCV RNA, for at least a year.

There is no vaccine against hepatitis C and it may prove difficult to develop one.[51]

References

1. Chan S-W, Simmonds P, McOmish F, Yap P-L, *et al.* Serological responses to infection with three different types of hepatitis C virus [letter]. *Lancet* 1991; **338**: 1391
2. Simmonds P, McOmish F, Yap P-L, Chan S-W, *et al.* Sequence variability in the 5' non-coding region of hepatitis C virus: identification of a new virus type and restrictions on sequence diversity. *Journal of General Virology* 1993; **74**: 661–8
3. Simmonds P, Holmes EC, Cha T-A, Chan S-W, *et al.* Classification of hepatitis C virus into six major genotypes and a series of subtypes by phylogenetic analysis of the NS-5 region. *Journal of General Virology* 1993; **74:** 2391–9
4. McOmish F, Chan S-W, Dow BC, Gillon J, *et al.* Detection of three types of hepatitis C virus in blood donors: investigation of type-specific differences in serologic reactivity and rate of alanine aminotransferase abnormalities. *Transfusion* 1993; **33**: 7–13
5. Alter HJ, Purcell RH, Shih JW, Melpolder JC, *et al.* Detection of antibody to hepatitis C virus in prospectively followed transfusion recipients with acute and chronic non-A,non-B hepatitis. *New England Journal of Medicine* 1989; **321**: 1494–500
6. Rassam SW, Dusheiko GM. Epidemiology and transmission of hepatitis C infection. *European Journal of Gastroenterology* 1991; **3**: 585–91
7. Thaler MM, Park C-K, Landers DV, Wara DW, *et al.* Vertical transmission of hepatitis C virus. *Lancet* 1991; **338**: 17–18
8. Lin H-H, Hsu H-Y, Chang M-H, Hong K-F, *et al.* Low prevalence of hepatitis C virus and infrequent perinatal or spouse infections in pregnant women in Taiwan. *Journal of Medical Virology* 1991; **35**: 237–40
9. Bamber M, Murray A, Arborgh BAM, *et al.* Short incubation non-A, non-B hepatitis transmitted by factor VIII concentrates in patients with congenital coagulation disorders. *Gut* 1981; **22**: 854–9
10. Lim SG, Lee CA, Charman H, Tilsed G, *et al.* Hepatitis C antibody assay in a longitudinal study of haemophiliacs. *British Journal of Haematology* 1991; **78**: 398–402
11. Nishioka K, Watanabe J, Furuta S, Tanaka E, *et al.* Antibody to the hepatitis C virus in acute hepatitis and chronic liver diseases in Japan. *Liver* 1991; **11**: 65–70

12. Esteban JI, Gonzalez A, Hernandez JM, Viladomiu L, *et al.* Evaluation of antibodies to hepatitis C virus in a study of transfusion-associated hepatitis. *New England Journal of Medicine* 1990; **323**: 1107–12
13. Farci P, Alter HJ, Wong D, Miller RH, *et al.* A long-term study of hepatitis C virus replication in non-A,non-B hepatitis *New England Journal of Medicine* 1991; **325**: 98–104
14. Patel A, Sherlock S, Dusheiko G, Scheuer PJ, *et al.* Clinical course and histological correlations in post-transfusion hepatitis C: the Royal Free Hospital experience. *European Journal of Gastroenterology and Hepatology* 1991; **3**: 491–5
15. Lee S-D, Hwang S-J, Lu R-H, Lai K-H, *et al.* Antibodies to hepatitis C virus in prospectively followed patients with post-transfusion hepatitis. *Journal of Infectious Diseases* 1991; **163**: 1354–7
16. Tanaka E, Kiyosawa K, Sodeyama T, Nakano Y, *et al.* Significance of antibody to hepatitis C virus in Japanese patients with viral hepatitis: relationship between anti-HCV antibody and the prognosis of non-A,non-B post-transfusion hepatitis. *Journal of Medical Virology* 1991; **33**: 117–22
17. Ogata N, Alter HJ, Miller RH, Purcell RH. Nucleotide sequence and mutation rate of the H strain of hepatitis C virus. *Proceedings of the National Academy of Sciences of the USA* 1991; **88**: 3392–6
18. Berman M, Alter HJ, Ishak KG, Purcell RH, Jones EA. The chronic sequelae of non-A,non-B hepatitis. *Annals of Internal Medicine* 1979; **91**: 1–6
19. Koretz RL, Stone O, Gitnick GL. The long term course of non-A,non-B post-transfusion hepatitis. *Gastroenterology* 1980; **79**: 893–8
20. Mattsson L, Weiland O, Glaumann H. Chronic non-A,non-B hepatitis developed after transfusions, illicit self-injections or sporadically: outcome during long-term follow-up—a comparison. *Liver* 1989; **9**: 120–7
21. Dammacco F, Sansonno D. Antibodies to hepatitis C virus in essential mixed cryoglobulinaemia [see comments]. *Clinical and Experimental Immunology* 1992; **87**: 352–6
22. Moldvay J, Deny P, Pol S, Brechot C, Lamas E. Detection of hepatitis C virus RNA in peripheral blood mononuclear cells of infected patients by *in situ* hybridization. *Blood* 1994; **83**: 269–73
23. Abe K, Kurata T, Shikata T, Sugitani M, Oda T. Experimental transmission of non-A,non-B hepatitis by saliva [letter]. *Journal of Infectious Diseases* 1987; **155**: 1078–109X
24. Zuckerman J, Clewley G, Griffiths P, Cockcroft A. Prevalence of hepatitis C antibodies in clinical health-care workers. *Lancet* 1994; **343**: 1618–20
25. Tabor E, Gerety RJ, Drucker JA, Seeff LB, *et al.* Transmission of non-A,non-B hepatitis from man to chimpanzee. *Lancet* 1978; **i**: 463–6
26. Thomas DL, Factor SH, Kelen GD, Washington AS, *et al.* Viral hepatitis in health care personnel at the Johns Hopkins Hospital: the seroprevalence of and risk factors for hepatitis B virus and hepatitis C virus infection. *Archives of Internal Medicine* 1993; **153**: 1705–12
27. Struve J, Aronsson B, Frenning B, Forsgren M, Weiland O. Prevalence of antibodies against hepatitis C virus infection among health care

workers in Stockholm. *Scandinavian Journal of Gastroenterology* 1994; **29**: 360–2

28. Klein RS, Freeman K, Taylor PE, Stevens CE. Occupational risk for hepatitis C virus infection among New York City dentists. *Lancet* 1991; **338**: 1539–42
29. Germanaud J, Causse X, Dhumeaux D. Transmission of hepatitis C by accidental needle-stick injury: evaluation of the risk. *Presse Medicale* 1994; **23**: 1078–82
30. Hernandez ME, Bruguera M, Puyuelo T, Barrera JM, *et al.* Risk of needle-stick injuries in the transmission of hepatitis C virus in hospital personnel. *Journal of Hepatology* 1992; **16**: 56–8
31. Mitsui T, Iwano K, Masuko K, Yamazaki C, *et al.* Hepatitis C virus infection in medical personnel after needlestick accident. *Hepatology* 1992; **16**: 1109–14
32. Kiyosawa K, Sodeyama T, Tanaka E, Nakano Y, *et al.* Hepatitis C in hospital employees with needlestick injuries. *Annals of Internal Medicine* 1991; **115**: 367–9
33. Marranconi F, Mecenero V, Pellizzer GP, Bettini MC, *et al.* HCV infection after accidental needlestick injury in health-care workers. *Infection* 1992; **20**: 111
34. Seeff LB. Hepatitis C from a needlestick injury [letter]. *Annals of Internal Medicine* 1991; **115**: 411
35. Vaglia A, Nicolin R, Puro V, Ippolito G, *et al.* Needlestick hepatitis C virus seroconversion in a surgeon. *Lancet* 1990; **336**: 1315–6
36. Sartori M, La Terra G, Aglietta M, Manzin A, *et al.* Transmission of hepatitis C via blood splash into conjunctiva. *Scandinavian Journal of Infectious Diseases* 1993; **25**: 270–1
37. Dusheiko GM, Smith M, Scheuer PJ. Hepatitis C virus transmitted by human bite [letter]. *Lancet* 1990; **336**: 503–4
38. Eyster ME, Alter HJ, Aledort LM, Quan S, *et al.* Heterosexual co-transmission of hepatitis C virus (HCV) and human immunodeficiency virus (HIV) *Annals of Internal Medicine* 1991; **115**: 764–8
39. Besman CK, Miller GB, Blumberg LH, Schoub BD. Hepatitis B virus transmission via Autolet guard [letter]. *South African Medical Journal* 1990; **77**: 654
40. Polish LB, Shapiro CN, Bauer F, Klotz P, *et al.* Nosocomial transmission of hepatitis B virus associated with the use of a spring-loaded finger-stick device. *New England Journal of Medicine* 1992; **326**: 721–5
41. Cariani E, Zonaro A, Primi D, Magni E, *et al.* Detection of HCV RNA and antibodies to HCV after needlestick injury [letter] *Lancet* 1991; **337**: 850
42. Abildgaard N, Peterslund NA. Hepatitis C virus transmitted by tattooing needle [letter]. *Lancet* 1991; **338**: 460
43. Niu MT, Alter MJ, Kristensen C, Margolis HS. Outbreak of hemodialysis-associated non-A,non-B hepatitis and correlation with antibody to hepatitis C virus. *American Journal of Kidney Diseases* 1992; **19**: 345–52
44. Bilgin N, Simsek H, Haberal M. Prevalence of anti-HCV positivity in hemodialysis and renal transplant patients at our center. *Transplantation Proceedings* 1993; **25**: 3261–2

45. Pereira BJG, Milford EL, Kirkman RL, Levey AS. Transmission of hepatitis C virus by organ transplantation. *New England Journal of Medicine* 1991; **325**: 454–60
46. Okamoto H, Sugiyama Y, Okada S, Kurai K, *et al.* Typing hepatitis C virus by polymerase chain reaction with type-specific primers: application to clinical surveys and tracing infectious sources. *Journal of General Virology* 1992; **73**: 673–9
47. Honda M, Kaneko S, Unoura M, Kobayashi K, Murakami S. Risk of hepatitis C virus infections through household contact with chronic carriers: analysis of nucleotide sequences. *Hepatology* 1993; **17**: 971–6
48. Davis JM, Demling RH, Lewis FR, Hoover E, Waymack JP. The Surgical Infection Society's policy on human immunodeficiency virus and hepatitis B and C infection: the *Ad Hoc* Committee on Acquired Immunodeficiency Syndrome and Hepatitis. *Archives of Surgery* 1992; **127**: 218–21
49. Hu DJ, Kane MA, Heymann DL. Transmission of HIV, hepatitis B virus, and other bloodborne pathogens in health care settings: a review of risk factors and guidelines for prevention. *Bulletin of the World Health Organisation* 1991; **69**: 623–30
50. Gerberding JL, Henderson DK. Management of occupational exposures to bloodborne pathogens: hepatitis B virus, hepatitis C virus, and human immunodeficiency virus. *Clinical Infectious Diseases* 1992; **14**: 1179–85
51. Choo Q-L, Kuo G, Ralston R, Weiner A, *et al.* Vaccination of chimpanzees against infection by the hepatitis C virus. *Proceedings of the National Academy of Sciences of the USA* 1994; **91**: 1294–8

4 | Tuberculosis

Craig Skinner
Consultant Physician/Senior Clinical Lecturer in Medicine, Heartlands Hospital and Chest Clinic, Birmingham, and University of Birmingham

---

Tuberculosis (TB) is a worldwide problem and globally there are more deaths from the disease—3 million per year—than from any other infection. The AIDS epidemic has added a new dimension, since TB is a major opportunistic infection and the only disease likely to be transmitted from an AIDS patient to family, carers or community. To compound the problem, multiple drug-resistant TB, mainly caused by poor treatment, has emerged in Asia, Africa, the Pacific and the USA. In truth the fight against TB is only beginning.

In the USA the incidence of TB has increased since 1985. The problem is concentrated in a number of large cities, for example New York where TB has reached epidemic proportions, and there the problem is linked to poverty, homelessness, immigration, AIDS and hard drug abuse. To make matters worse the resources and expertise which had been developed to control the disease have been eroded in recent times in the mistaken belief that TB was a disease of the past. We must not make that same mistake in Britain.

In England and Wales, after decades of decline, there has been a small but steady increase in notifications of TB since 1987 (Fig 1) and now there are about 6,000 new cases per year with 350 deaths, the latter mainly in older people. This increase in incidence is thought to be due to a combination of new immigration, unemployment, poverty, homelessness and changes in the age structure of high risk ethnic groups but there is no evidence that HIV infection has so far had any appreciable effect.[1] The 1993 National Survey of TB notifications in England and Wales, still in the final stages of its data collection, is intended to help clarify the reasons for the increase and the role of HIV infection.

In Britain drug resistant TB is currently a small problem[2] and multiple drug resistance occurs in only a handful of patients.

The key to successful TB control is screening of at-risk groups to identify cases (notably those which are infectious) and then providing curative treatment. Only smear-positive pulmonary cases

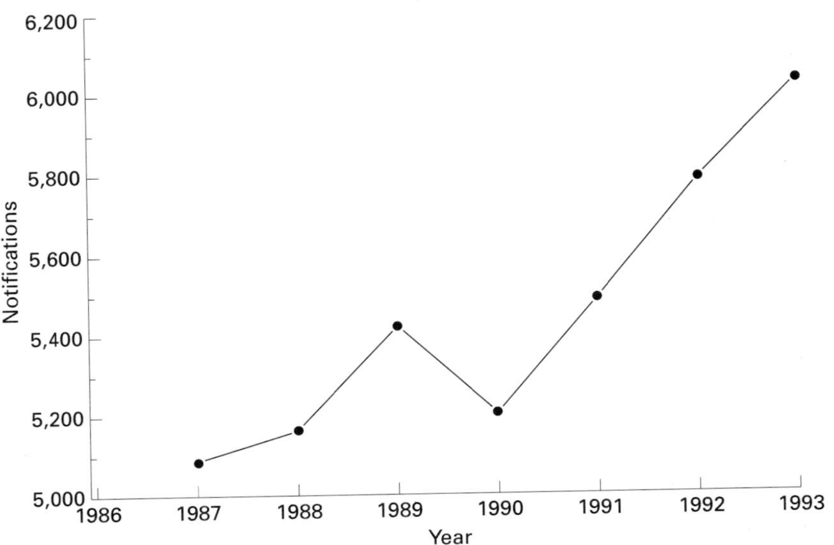

Fig 1. *Tuberculosis notifications in England and Wales (OPCS survey)*

are infectious and become non-infectious after 2 weeks of chemotherapy, remaining so if adequate medication is continued and completed. In addition to finding cases for treatment, screening will also detect those infected but not diseased, who may receive chemoprophylaxis or follow-up, and those uninfected who may receive BCG vaccination.

Risks to health care workers

Tuberculous infection is acquired by inhalation of bacilli in tiny airborne droplets. In the health care setting this usually arises from repeated, close contact with patients who have smear-positive pulmonary disease, or with infected laboratory specimens or post-mortem material. Among healthy close contacts of an infectious case, no more than one-sixth become infected and, of these, the lifetime risk of developing disease is only 10–15%. The risk to fit health care workers should therefore not be overemphasised—it is now rare for them to acquire tuberculosis from their patients.

TB is a prescribed occupational disease for health care workers. However, routine statistical information does not enable its incidence in health care workers to be monitored, so that special surveys are necessary. These show that at one time TB was much commoner in at-risk health care workers in the UK than in the general population. For example, medical laboratory staff had up to a ninefold risk in 1949–53,[3] and a fivefold risk in the 1970s.[4] However, a study in England and Wales in the 1980s[5] showed that the incidence was similar to or lower than that of the general population for all occupational groups except mortuary attendants, whilst a Scottish study[6] showed similar findings, with only medical laboratory technicians having an increased incidence. The risk to mortuary workers was again highlighted more recently.[7]

A region-wide surveillance system for TB in hospital workers has been set up in the West Midlands[8] with case ascertainment via both the occupational health record and the Midland Thoracic Society Rare Diseases Register to which any case of TB in NHS staff is routinely notified by the treating chest physician. Preliminary results to date suggest that, with the possible exception of mortuary staff, TB is no more common in NHS staff than in the working age population.

Multiple drug resistant TB (MDR-TB) in health care workers

MDR-TB is neither more nor less infectious than drug sensitive TB, but it is more difficult to treat and is therefore more serious when transmitted. In the USA several MDR-TB outbreaks have occurred, mainly in hospital AIDS units, but most of the patients and many of the affected health care workers were dually infected with HIV and TB (Table 1).

An AIDS patient exposed to infectious TB has a high risk of being infected, a much higher risk of developing TB if infected—at least 50%, and will develop the disease quickly, often

Table 1. HIV-associated multiple drug resistant tuberculosis outbreaks

Facility	Location	Year	Number of cases	HIV infection (%)
Hospital A	Miami	1990	65	93
Hospital B	New York City	1990	35	100*
Hospital C	New York City	1991–1992	70	94
Hospital D	New York City	1991	29	91
Hospital E	New York State	1991	7	20
Hospital F	New York City	1992	16	82
Hospital G	New Jersey	1992	13	100
Prison system	New York State	1991–1992	42	91

Modified from Villarino ME, Geiter LJ, Simone BM. *Public Health Reports* 1992;**107**:616–25.
*HIV infection in case definition.

in weeks rather than months or years. Hence an outbreak of TB in AIDS patients is explosive; if in addition the source cases are multiple drug resistant, the problem becomes very serious. In the USA this has led to recommendations for strict infection control including detention of uncompliant patients, initial treatment in isolation rooms with negative pressure, frequent air-change ventilation, germicidal ultraviolet radiation, and powered air respirators ('Darth Vader masks') for attending nurses and doctors.[9]

In contrast to the USA, the overlap between HIV infection and TB infection in the UK is, at least at present, much less, each infection tending to occur in different groups in the population. Furthermore MDR-TB is not presently a significant problem in the UK, and no USA-type outbreaks have yet been described. Finally, BCG vaccination is not routinely offered to health care workers in the USA, although a recent decision analysis[10] suggested that this might be a more cost-effective protective measure than the current practice of repeated tuberculin testing followed by chemoprophylaxis for convertors.

Control measures

These are designed to protect staff in contact with patients and laboratory specimens, to protect susceptible patients by detecting infectious TB in staff, and to protect the employer (from litigation). It is helpful to have a local policy jointly agreed by the occupational health department, chest medical service and control of infection team. Control measures comprise:

1. Screening new and existing staff to detect TB.
2. Protection of staff by BCG vaccination.
3. Infection control measures.

Figure 2 is a flow chart encapsulating screening and vaccination recommendations for new staff at the pre-employment stage.

Screening new staff

Measures include recording any symptoms of TB, details of previous BCG vaccination along with the presence or absence of a BCG scar, and tuberculin skin testing (preferably the Heaf test) or chest x-ray where indicated.

Routine pre-employment chest radiography is a waste of time and money.[11] The current (1990) British Thoracic Society guidelines[12] recommend that x-ray be restricted to those with a strongly

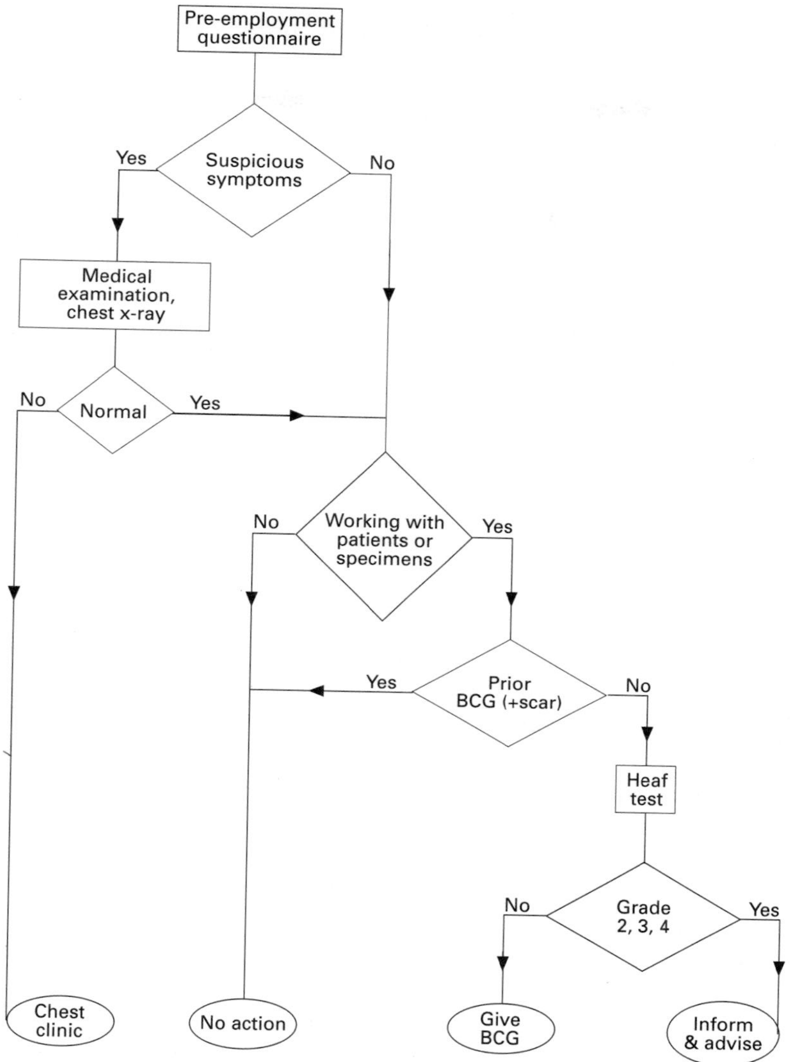

Fig 2. *Protection of NHS staff; pre-employment measures*

positive tuberculin test and the number of pre-employment x-rays undertaken has thereby been substantially reduced. However, a further reduction is still possible because there is now evidence from studies in London[13,14] and Birmingham[8] that strongly positive tuberculin skin reactions are common in health care workers, with or without BCG scars, and in asymptomatic workers are not indicative of active TB or predictive of chest x-ray abnormalities. Hence pre-employment chest x-ray should be reserved for people with suspicious symptoms—persistent cough, unexplained weight loss, malaise and night sweats.

Heaf testing is only necessary in those who do not have a convincing BCG scar, which can be taken as evidence of satisfactory vaccination.

Symptomless individuals with grade 2, 3 or 4 positive Heaf tests should be advised that they may have encountered the tubercle bacillus in the past, do not require BCG and should report any future suspicious symptoms. Occasionally a chest x-ray may be considered necessary, for example in an individual from a high-risk country especially if he/she is to work with children or immunocompromised patients.

The 1994 revision of the British Thoracic Society guidelines will reflect these suggested changes in policy and practice.

Surveillance of existing staff

Routine periodic chest radiography is not necessary for any group of health care staff and is not effective in early detection of tuberculosis because most staff who develop TB present with symptoms. All health care workers should be aware of the possible symptoms of TB and of the importance of reporting these promptly, but an annual questionnaire sent to at-risk staff is unproductive.[8] Special arrangements may be advisable for mortuary staff who appear to be a high risk group. The occupational health department should be notified of any mortuary worker who is off sick for more than 2 weeks, and surveillance for TB in mortuary staff may usefully be combined with annual surveillance for adverse effects of aldehyde exposure.

BCG vaccination

Those who are Heaf-negative on pre-employment screening should be offered BCG vaccination, irrespective of age. In older persons some units may first prefer to repeat the Heaf test to detect a boosted reaction and avoid unnecessary vaccination. The BCG vaccination site should be inspected after 6 weeks and those without a satisfactory reaction should be given a further Heaf test with a second vaccination if this is negative. If BCG is declined by a member of staff the risks should be fully explained and the refusal recorded.

Table 2. Action following detection of infectious TB on a general ward

Action	Responsibility
Notify case	Chest consultant
Advise other patients' consultants and GPs	Control of infection committee
Reassure/advise staff contacts Treat as close contact* if • immunocompromised staff member • index case highly infectious • unusually close contact – mouth-to-mouth resuscitation – repeated chest physiotherapy – prolonged care of dependent patient	Occupational health department

*Heaf test at 2 months. If grade 3/4, x-ray and repeat at 3 and 12 months.

Infection control measures

Only patients with smear-positive pulmonary disease should be regarded as infectious. If the organisms are fully sensitive, patients become non-infectious after 2 weeks of chemotherapy including rifampicin and isoniazid. Hence such patients should be segregated for 2 weeks after starting chemotherapy in a single room vented to the air outside the building and the door should be kept shut as much as possible. Ideally the room should be ventilated by a mechanical extract system, without recirculation, which exhausts to a safe location. Bottled sputum specimens should be transmitted in plastic bags labelled 'biohazard' and infected material should be incinerated. However, barrier nursing is unnecessary and staff need not wear gowns or masks. More rigorous measures may be indicated particularly for HIV units or for those with multiple drug resistant organisms.[15] The need for these additional measures must be decided on the basis of a risk assessment by individual units treating HIV and/or multiple drug resistant TB patients.

It is not unusual for a patient in a general ward to be diagnosed as having infectious tuberculosis, sometimes after a delay of several days. Suggested action to be taken in these circumstances is shown in Table 2 and examples of suitable letters to staff in contact and to the consultants/GPs of patients in contact are in Figs 3 and 4.

HIV and protection of health care staff against TB

HIV infection is relevant both to staff vaccination and to staff risk of contracting TB at work. It is recommended in the UK that BCG

Dear

There has been a patient on the ward where you have been working who has been found to have infectious TB.

Your BCG given on (date) will have given you immunity/When we checked your Heaf test on (date) it showed that you have immunity.

However very occasionally people can catch TB after they have been shown to have some immunity. If you are ill and consult your GP or need treatment or investigations in hospital within the next 12 months, please mention your contact with TB.

If you have chest symptoms or cough for more than two weeks, or unexplained illness and fever, please come to the Occupational Health Department for advice.

Please take this letter to your GP.

If you have any queries or worries about this please contact the Occupational Health Department.

Fig 3. *Letter to staff after casual exposure to infectious tuberculosis*

vaccination should not be given to any individual known or suspected to be HIV infected.[16] Screening for HIV infection of new staff is inappropriate, but routine enquiries will include questions to determine if the individual may be immunocompromised. Staff should be encouraged to report HIV infection to the occupational health department so that advice about any necessary modifica-

Dear Dr

Re: Contact with 'Open' Pulmonary Tuberculosis

During the first week in (month) a number of your patients were on Ward X at the same time as John Doe who turns out to have infectious tuberculosis. It must be assumed that patients and staff in contact with Mr Doe have been exposed to *M. tuberculosis.* Patients in your care on the relevant ward during Mr Doe's admission are listed below, and I enclose for each patient an adhesive label with the information that they have been exposed to *M. tuberculosis.* Although the risk of transmission to patients may be small, I would be grateful if the label could be placed in the patient's medical record so that this can be borne in mind on follow-up.

PATIENT'S NAME	HOSPITAL NUMBER
JOHN KEATS	12345
FREDERIC CHOPIN	67890

Fig 4. *Letter to consultant of patient casually exposed to infectious tuberculosis*

tions to their work can be given. A move away from work with high risks of infection should be offered as they become immunocompromised.

About 6% of AIDS patients develop tuberculosis. A high index of suspicion is necessary and infection control measures, as previously described, are important. In addition, a policy of minimal staff presence with adequate ventilation during activities likely to induce coughing, such as inhaling pentamidine, sputum induction and bronchoscopy, should be instituted.

Deficiencies in current practice

There are a number of deficiencies in the management of the TB risk to health care staff. These include:

1. Wasteful procedures, such as unnecessary pre-employment chest x-rays or Heaf tests, are still carried out.
2. Staff may evade screening and protective measures.[17] Doctors are notorious in this regard, and having acquired TB during their training years may transmit the disease to their patients.
3. Record keeping is sometimes poor. This may prevent adequate defence of a legal action against an employer brought by a member of staff who develops TB.
4. There is no systematic monitoring of the incidence of TB in health care workers.

The future

The way ahead for the next few years is rigorous application of the present, proven measures though there are promising developments in both diagnosis and treatment which may affect future practice. Methods of identifying tubercle bacilli and their drug sensitivity in hours or days, rather than weeks, are likely to be introduced into routine clinical practice in the next 5 years. Those being developed are based on the polymerase chain reaction (PCR), restriction fragment length polymorphism (RFLP) which also allows DNA fingerprinting, and chemiluminescence. They will allow more rapid and effective treatment further limiting the small risk of transmission of TB, including MDR-TB, to health care workers.

Effective treatments shorter than 6 months are needed. Preliminary results of a combination of drugs and a vaccine derived from *Mycobacterium vaccae* are encouraging. There are no prospects in the immediate future of a better preventive vaccine than BCG.

References

1. Watson JM, Meredith SK, Whitmore-Overton E, Bannister B, Darbyshire JH. Tuberculosis and HIV: estimates of the overlap in England and Wales. *Thorax* 1993; **48**: 199–203
2. Warburton ARE, Jenkins PA, Waight PA, Watson JM. Drug resistance in initial isolates of *Mycobacterium tuberculosis* in England and Wales 1982–1991. *Communicable Disease Report* 1993; **3**: R175–9
3. Reid DD. Incidence of tuberculosis among workers in medical laboratories. *British Medical Journal* 1957; **ii**: 10–14
4. Harrington JM, Shannon HS. Incidence of tuberculosis, hepatitis, brucellosis and shigellosis in British medical laboratory workers. *British Medical Journal* 1976; **i**: 759–62
5. Lunn JA, Mayho V. Incidence of pulmonary tuberculosis by occupation of hospital employees in the National Health Service in England and Wales 1980–84. *Journal of the Society of Occupational Medicine* 1989; **39**: 30–2
6. Capewell S, Leaker AR, Leitch AG. Pulmonary tuberculosis in health service staff—is it still a problem? *Tubercle* 1988; **69**: 113–8
7. Grist NR, Emslie JAN. Infections in British clinical laboratories. *Journal of Clinical Pathology* 1991; **44**: 667–9
8. Burge A, Kumar S, Skinner C. Control of tuberculosis in NHS staff: West Midlands 1990–92. *Thorax* 1992; **48**: 463
9. Voelker R. New federal stances on TB control may be confusing to health care facilities. *Journal of the American Medical Association* 1993; **270**: 1903–4
10. Greenberg PD, Lax KG, Schechter CB. Tuberculosis in house staff: a decision analysis comparing the tuberculin screening strategy with the BCG vaccination. *American Review of Respiratory Disease* 1991; **143**: 490–5
11. Jachuck SJ, Bound CL, Jones CE, Bryson M. Is a pre-employment chest radiograph necessary for NHS employees? *British Medical Journal* 1988; **296**: 1187–8
12. Joint Tuberculosis Committee of the British Thoracic Society. Control and prevention of tuberculosis in Britain: an updated code of practice *British Medical Journal* 1990; **300**: 995–9
13. Chaturvedi N, Cockcroft A. Tuberculosis screening in health service employees: who needs chest x-rays? *Occupational Medicine* 1992; **42**: 179–82
14. Madan I. Pre-employment chest radiograph for health service staff: who needs it? *British Medical Journal* 1993; **306**: 1041–2
15. American Thoracic Society. Control of tuberculosis in the United States. *American Review of Respiratory Disease* 1992; **146**: 1623–33
16. Joint Tuberculosis Committee of the British Thoracic Society. Guidelines on the management of tuberculosis and HIV infection in the United Kingdom. *British Medical Journal* 1992; **304**: 1231–3
17. Clague JE, Fields P, Graham DR, Davies PDO. Screening for tuberculosis: current practices and attitudes of hospital workers. *Tubercle* 1991; **72**: 265–7

5 | Allergic respiratory disease

Anthony J Newman Taylor
Consultant Physician, Royal Brompton Hospital, and Professor of Occupational & Environmental Medicine, National Heart & Lung Institute, London

---

Of the three patterns of allergic respiratory disease—asthma, allergic bronchopulmonary mycosis and extrinsic allergic alveolitis—only asthma, on occasions accompanied by rhinitis, conjunctivitis and urticaria, is an important problem for health care professionals. Asthma caused by sensitisation to an agent inhaled at work (hypersensitivity induced asthma) is the most frequent category of occupational lung disease reported to the Surveillance of Work and Occupational Respiratory Disease (SWORD) scheme, to which the great majority of respiratory and occupational physicians report *new* cases of occupational lung disease. The number of new cases reported in 1993 was an estimated 3,500, of which asthma accounted for 28%.[1] From January 1989 to December 1993 there were 107 notified cases of asthma in health care workers (Table 1). These do not include cases reported from the pharmaceutical industry (primarily caused by antibiotics and laboratory animals) or from research laboratory staff (primarily caused by laboratory animals). During the same 4 years, 116 cases of asthma caused by laboratory animals in research and technical laboratory staff were reported to SWORD.

In a recent review, Hayes and Fitzgerald listed the causes of occupational asthma in health care workers reported in the medical literature (Table 2).[2] Evidence that high molecular weight proteins had caused asthma came from (a) a history of asthma, usually accompanied by rhinitis, conjunctivitis or urticaria, following exposure to the high molecular weight protein, (b) a history of work-related asthma, improving when away from work—at weekends and on holidays—and recurring during the working week, and (c) evidence of specific IgE antibody to the high molecular weight protein, from either an immediate skin prick response or identification by immunoassay of specific IgE in serum. For low molecular weight agents, evidence of specific IgE antibody was usually not present; objective evidence of cause and effect was

Table 1. Asthma in 107 health care workers (January 1989 to December 1993; reported to SWORD)

Occupation	Substance
Physicians (4)	Histamine; formaldehyde; glutaraldehyde; trypsin
Dentists (4)	Aerosols from drilling (2); glutaraldehyde; unknown
Nurses (68)	Glutaraldehyde (40); cleaning products (7); formaldehyde (3); latex (3); rubber gloves (2); isocyanate (2); antibiotics (2); colophony in flexible collodion (2); bone cement; pig abattoir antigens; 58frekaderm spray; new hospital building; pancrex; sorbisan dressing
Radiographers (11)	Glutaraldehyde (3); fixer (3); latex; acetic acid; processor fumes; sulphur dioxide; unknown
Physiotherapists (1)	Glutaraldehyde
Operating theatre/ ward assistants/ nursing auxiliaries (5)	Glutaraldehyde (3); wood sealant; cleaning products
Plaster orderlies (2)	Isocyanate (plaster casts) (2)
Dental nurses/assistants (7)	Glutaraldehyde (5); alginates; butyl methacrylate
TSSU assistant (1)	Cotton dust
Porter (1)	Pigeons
Hospital laboratory staff (3)	Glutaraldehyde; formaldehyde; cotton wool

primarily provided by the demonstration that the chemical, in concentrations less than those toxic for mucosal surfaces, provoked an (often late) asthmatic response.

There is little information about the prevalence of sensitisation or asthma in different occupational groups (eg medical or nursing staff, radiographers, physiotherapists, laboratory staff), the circumstances in which disease occurs, the relative importance of its different causes, or the consequences of developing asthma. Four causes of occupational asthma have attracted particular attention: formaldehyde, glutaraldehyde, latex and psyllium.

Formaldehyde was one of the earliest agents widely encountered by health service staff to be reported as causing asthma. Sterilisation with glutaraldehyde and the use of latex rubber gloves have increased, especially with concern over the transmission of human

Table 2. Causes of occupational asthma in health care workers[2]

Substance	Occupation
High molecular weight	
Animal proteins	Laboratory workers
Psyllium (ispaghula)	Nurse
Pancreatic extracts	Nurse
Bromelain	Laboratory technician
Bovine serum albumin	Laboratory technician
Latex	Nurse
'Allergen exposure'	Technician
Corn starch (rubber glove)	Obstetrician
Low molecular weight	
Formaldehyde	Nurse
Glutaraldehyde	Nurse; radiographer
Hexachlorophene	Nurse
Chloramine	Laboratory technician
Methyl methacrylate	Theatre nurse
Methyl blue	Nurse; ECG technician
Enflurane	Anaesthetist
Isonicotinic acid hydrazide	Hospital pharmacist
Chlorhexidine	Auxiliary nurse; midwife
Sulphathiazoles	Nurse
Terpene (rubber glove)	Laboratory technician
X-ray fixative/developer	Radiographer

immunodeficiency virus (HIV) and hepatitis B virus. Allergy to psyllium, widely used as a bulk fibre laxative, has been investigated both during its manufacture and in hospital staff. Occupational allergy and asthma in those sensitised to latex and psyllium pose the threat of severe allergic reactions on subsequent encounters, which can occur in a therapeutic setting.

Formaldehyde and glutaraldehyde

Formaldehyde is a low molecular weight chemical which has been used for many years as a fixative in anatomy and histopathology departments and more recently as a sterilising agent in renal dialysis units. Five of the 107 cases reported to SWORD from 1989 to 1993 were attributed to formaldehyde: one physician, three nurses and one hospital laboratory worker.

Hendrick and Lane reported two cases of asthma induced by

formaldehyde among 28 staff in a renal dialysis unit where it was used to sterilise the equipment.[3] In both cases, test inhalation of formaldehyde reproducibly provoked a late asthmatic response which in one case was followed by nocturnal asthma that recurred on five subsequent nights.

Nordman reported 12 cases of asthma caused by formaldehyde in 230 persons all occupationally exposed to it, though none was a health care worker.[4] In 11 of them an asthmatic response was provoked in an inhalation test by an airborne concentration of formaldehyde of 2.5 mg/m^3 and in one by 1.2 mg/m^3. Three of the 12 cases had no measurable airway responsiveness before formaldehyde exposure, whereas 71 of the 218 in whom formaldehyde did not provoke an asthmatic response had increased airway responsiveness to inhaled histamine. In six cases formaldehyde provoked a late asthmatic response. The late asthmatic responses provoked by formaldehyde and the lack of immediate responses provoked by formaldehyde in cases of asthma with hyperresponsive airways make it unlikely that these were irritant reactions and more likely asthma induced by hypersensitivity to formaldehyde.

It is unclear how frequently formaldehyde induces asthma. Only five of the 107 cases reported in health care workers from 1989 to 1993 were attributed to formaldehyde, and the 12 cases reported by Nordman were drawn from a highly selected population of 230 persons referred during 6½ years with suspected formaldehyde induced asthma from throughout Finland.

In contrast, glutaraldehyde was reported to SWORD as the cause of asthma in 55 of the 107 cases in health care workers: 40 hospital nurses, 5 dental nurses, 3 radiographers, 3 operating theatre staff, a physician, a dentist, a physiotherapist and a hospital laboratory worker. However, the number of cases reported in the medical literature in whom the diagnosis has been validated by inhalation testing is very few. Inhalation of glutaraldehyde provoked an asthmatic response in a radiographer[5] and in one of four endoscopy nurses investigated for symptoms suggestive of asthma caused by glutaraldehyde.[6] Waldron suggested that the results of his survey of nurses exposed to glutaraldehyde in a London teaching hospital were more consistent with an irritant than an allergic response.[7]

Psyllium

Psyllium is widely used as a concentrated fibre source in bulk laxatives and cereals. It is the seed husk of the *Plantago ovata* and more than 7,000 tonnes are imported into the USA each year. Inhalation of psyllium dust causes allergy in its manufacturers and in health care workers. Cases have evidence of specific IgE to proteins from the seed embryo and endosperm contaminating the husk in the pharmaceutical product. Malo *et al,* in a survey of the 248 staff of four chronic care hospitals in Quebec where psyllium was regularly dispensed,[8] identified occupational asthma in 4% and specific IgE by skin prick testing in 5% and by RAST in 12%. From this prevalence figure, they estimated that there could be some 800 cases of occupational asthma among the 20,000 chronic care hospital staff in Quebec.

Unlike most causes of occupational asthma, where exposure is limited to the work place, psyllium may be encountered also when prescribed as a laxative and as a cholesterol lowering agent under the name Heartwise. James *et al* reported 20 cases of allergic reactions to Heartwise;[9] 17 had asthma, 14 had urticaria and 9 diarrhoea and vomiting, within 2–20 minutes of ingesting it, and all 20 had specific IgE to psyllium. Fifteen of the 20 had previously dispensed psyllium, 14 as nurses, and 11 had experienced symptoms when doing so.

Latex

Recognition of allergy to latex has increased dramatically in the past 5 years, primarily because of its increasing incidence, particularly in the USA, following the greatly increased use of rubber gloves by health care staff to reduce the risk of infection with hepatitis B virus and HIV.

Latex is the milky sap of the tree *Hevea brasiliensis.* Raw latex is used in a variety of products which include surgical gloves, balloons, condoms and catheters. The allergens identified in latex have molecular weights of 14, 28 and 88 kD to which specific IgE in the serum of sensitised individuals binds. The majority of cases are probably sensitised by the inhalation of the dusting powder from the gloves which has adsorbed these latex proteins. Swanson *et al* found 13–21 ng/m^3 of airborne latex allergens in areas of a hospital where rubber gloves were regularly used and 0.3–1.8 ng/m^3 in areas where they were rarely used.[10] They also identified 34 cases of latex allergy among 49 Mayo Clinic employees; the majority were nurses and laboratory technicians, and all had jobs that involved changing of latex gloves several times each day. Contact with skin provoked urticaria and inhalation, rhinitis and asthma. A recent study reported the prevalence of latex allergy among the 273 staff of a hospital in Belgium.[11] Thirteen (4.7%) had an immediate skin test response to latex; all 13 had a history of contact urticaria, 12 of rhinitis and conjunctivitis, and 5 had asthma. Inhalation tests with latex provoked an asthmatic response in 7 (2.5%).

Latex allergy is of concern because of the risks of latex exposure at work and because of the high risk posed by subsequent exposure, often hidden, both to latex and to cross-reacting allergens in other substances. Rubber tree plants and weeping fig can provoke reactions in latex sensitive individuals, as can several foods including avocado, banana and chestnuts.[12] Natural latex is also a constituent of many rubber tyres; a recent study identified latex allergens in urban airborne particles, presumably derived from degrading rubber tyres.[13] However, the greatest potential risk to the latex sensitive individual is contact, often outside the place of work, which may provoke an anaphylactic reaction. Jaeger *et al* reported 70 patients with latex allergy, all health care workers, of whom 54% were nurses or technicians and 37% physicians or medical students.[14] Four of these cases had experienced anaphylactic reactions, provoked by glove contact in one case, a gynaecological examination in another, condom use in another and the use of a rubber-coated squash racket in the fourth. Because of the risk to latex sensitive individuals from gloves worn by staff during an examination or operation, Bubak *et al* made specific recommendations for their protection (Table 3).[15]

Table 3. Specific recommendations for latex sensitive persons[15]

- Use vinyl gloves
- Use hypoallergenic latex gloves
- Request that co-workers use vinyl or hypoallergenic latex gloves
- Wear a medical identification tag
- Warn all health care providers of sensitivity and ask them to eliminate or minimise use of latex

For persons with anaphylactic reactivity to latex

- Carry and know how to use an adrenaline-containing emergency kit

Management

Occupationally induced respiratory allergy is an important and potentially preventable cause of ill-health and disability in health care workers. The basis of effective management, as with other causes of occupational allergy and asthma, is avoidance of further exposure to the cause. Where possible this should aim to allow affected individuals to continue their work by change such as substitution (eg of psyllium by a non-allergenic alternative laxative) or by effective process enclosure (eg of glutaraldehyde sterilisation).

Frequently such changes are not feasible and avoidance of exposure requires a change of work or, on occasion, job loss with its social and financial consequences. Health care workers are also at risk of unrecognised exposures outside their place of work, particularly in a therapeutic setting. To prevent such occurrences, which may be life threatening, they should be warned of the circumstances in which unrecognised exposure may occur, both medical (eg same drug but different name and indication) and non-medical (eg food and plants which may provoke reactions in latex allergic individuals). They should be advised to inform their medical advisers of the agents to which they are allergic and the potential consequences of re-exposure. Medical staff when asking patients about drug allergies should also ask past and present health care workers (and pharmaceutical and laboratory workers) about any drugs to which they have become sensitised in their work and of allergy to rubber gloves.

References

1. Sallie B, Meredith SK, Ross D, McDonald JC. SWORD '93. Surveillance of work-related and occupational respiratory disease in the UK. *Occupational Medicine* 1994; **44**: 177–82
2. Hayes JP, Fitzgerald MK. Occupational asthma among health care personnel: a cause for concern? *Thorax* 1994; **49**: 198–200
3. Hendrick DJ, Lane DJ. Occupational formalin asthma. *British Journal of Industrial Medicine* 1977; **34**: 11–8
4. Nordman H. Formaldehyde asthma—rare or overlooked? *Journal of Allergy and Clinical Immunology* 1985; **75**: 91–9
5. Cullinan P, Hayes J, Cannon J, Madan I, *et al.* Occupational asthma in radiographers [letter]. *Lancet* 1992; **340**: 1477
6. Corrado OJ, Osman J, Davies RH. Asthma and rhinitis after exposure to glutaraldehyde in endoscopy units. *Human Toxicology* 1986; **5**: 325–7
7. Waldron HA. Glutaraldehyde allergy in hospital workers [letter]. *Lancet* 1992; **339**: 880
8. Malo JL, Cartier A, L'Archeveque J, Lagier F, *et al.* Prevalence of

occupational asthma and immunologic sensitisation to psyllium among health personnel in chronic care hospitals. *American Review of Respiratory Disease* 1990; **142**: 1359–66

9. James JM, Cooke SK, Barett A, Sampson HA. Anaphylactic reactions to a psyllium containing cereal. *Journal of Allergy and Clinical Immunology* 1991; **88**: 402–8
10. Swanson MC, Bubak ME, Hunt LW, Reed CR. Occupational respiratory disease from latex [abstract]. *Journal of Allergy and Clinical Immunology* 1992; **89**: A227
11. Vandenplas O, Delwiche JP, Evrard G, Aimont P, *et al.* Prevalence of occupational asthma due to latex among hospital personnel. *American Journal of Respiratory and Critical Care Medicine* 1995; **151**: 54–60
12. Blanco C, Carrillo T, Queralto J, Cuevas M. Avocado hypersensitivity. *Allergy* 1994; **49**: 54–9
13. Brock Williams P, Buhr MP, Weber RW, Volz MA, *et al.* Latex allergy in respirable particular air pollution. *Journal of Allergy and Clinical Immunology* 1995; **95**: 88–95
14. Jaeger D, Kleinhans D, Czuppon AB, Baur X. Latex-specific proteins causing immediate-type cutaneous, nasal, bronchial and systemic reactions. *Journal of Allergy and Clinical Immunology* 1992; **89**: 759–68
15. Bubak ME, Reed CE, Fransway AF, Yunginger JW, *et al.* Allergic reactions to latex in health-care workers. *Mayo Clinic Proceedings* 1992; **67**: 1075–9

PART 2

Mental health aspects

RACHEL JENKINS
Mental Health, Elderly, Disability and Ethics Policy Branch, Department of Health

---

It is a great pleasure to be asked to write the introduction to the mental health section of this important and timely book on health risks to the health care professional. The chapters it contains represent authoritative reviews by key practitioners in the field, who identify and describe the alarming catalogue of health risks faced by health professionals, the precise extent of the morbidity and mortality resulting from these risks, and the human and economic costs they impose on society.

The Health of the Nation[1] has flagged up the central importance of fostering the health of the NHS workforce. The NHS is the nation's largest employer and thus has a unique opportunity to set a practical example of valuing both the mental and physical health of its employees. Workplace health policies should therefore not only address physical health, alcohol and drug misuse and AIDS, but also mental health. Such policies need the commitment of all levels of the organisation if they are to be effective.

If we are to make a serious attempt at reducing morbidity and mortality in health professionals, then we need a concerted programme of integrated action that includes mental health promotion, primary, secondary and tertiary prevention, and prevention of mortality.

Relevant mental health promotion consists of educating health care professionals in general skills which will promote mental health, such as regular physical exercise, stress management techniques, time management and the importance of caring for themselves.

Primary preventive action includes support targeted at high risk groups. Such support can be built into the organisation via regular supportive constructive appraisals for health care professionals in training, and for those in highly demanding posts. It also includes organisational developments to minimise the stress load on health care workers by appropriate competency-based training, management of long hours etc.

Secondary prevention includes prompt detection and management of illness, particularly anxiety and depression. This will include education of line managers to spot the early symptoms, and the provision of adequate occupational health resources to access the necessary counselling, diagnosis and management. In this context it is important to remember that many health care professionals, particularly doctors, do not routinely register with a GP and this severely impedes their access to appropriate health care when needed. Furthermore, 'corridor consultations' with colleagues may be positively dangerous in that they do not allow for a holistic assessment of the problems.

Tertiary prevention includes adequate rehabilitation back to work after a period of prolonged illness. Such rehabilitation is in the best interests of the organisation and the professional in that it avoids the costly process of early retirement, loss of valuable decades of experience and the costs of replacing that experience.

Prevention of suicide in health care professionals will depend firstly on an appreciation of the size of the problem by the health care profession itself so that its members are alerted to the risks when caring for one of their colleagues. Careful assessment of suicidal risk remains a vital cornerstone of good practice in consultations with health care professionals.

The interventions described above need to be accompanied by a change in the culture in which we train our health care professionals, so that we positively encourage the traits of taking good care of oneself and being able to acknowledge when we are tired, exhausted and in need of help. However, so long as such traits are regarded as 'wimpish', the heavy burden of morbidity and mortality will continue to take its toll. The educators of our undergraduates and graduates together with line managers have the opportunity to start the process of change that is necessary to make the nation's health care professionals a mentally healthy workforce.

1 Department of Health. *The Health of the Nation: The Strategy for Health in England*. London: HMSO, 1992.

6 | Burnout and alcohol problems

Desmond Kelly
Medical Director, The Priory Hospital, London

Never before have so many school leavers wanted to go into medicine, and yet the number of doctors wanting to leave medicine for other careers or take early retirement has probably never been higher. At the United Medical Schools of St Thomas's and Guy's in 1992 there were 11,700 applicants to become medical students and in 1993 there were 21,000 applicants for 200 places. The successful candidates can expect from their medical careers a great deal of stress and for some both disillusionment and burnout.

Morale in medicine

A questionnaire conducted by *Doctor* and *Hospital Doctor*, and reported on 24 June 1993, elicited 5,000 replies. The results indicate the present level of stress in medical practice.

1. Stress levels have risen 40% since the introduction of NHS reforms with two in five doctors now suffering to some extent.
2. Hospital doctors' morale is so low that one in three want to quit medicine and 48% are considering early retirement.
3. The most decisive response of all related to the effect on families about whom 88% of doctors said changes must be made to lower work-related stress.

This chapter offers some observations on stress and how to prevent burnout from the perspective of a practising clinical psychiatrist.

Statistics relating to medical practitioners

Doctors have twice as many road accidents as the general population, are three times more likely to have cirrhosis or to commit suicide, and are at least 30 times more likely to be addicted to drugs. They are 2.5 times more likely to be admitted to a psychiatric hospital; particularly common is hospitalisation for depression, alcoholism and drug addiction. It has been estimated that 3,000 general practitioners are alcoholics. General practitioners also have a high incidence of unresolved marital conflict and emotional problems.

The practice of medicine makes doctors particularly vulnerable to stress-related disorders and consequently to professional burnout. The most dedicated, committed, enthusiastic and idealistic are the most vulnerable.

Junior house officers surveyed in 1987 indicated a high level of distress. Overwork (91 hours per week on average) was reported as the most stressful aspect of their duties. Emotional disturbance was reported by 50%, depression by 28%, heavy drinking by 20%, and the use of medication for physical illness by 25%. The most empathic were found to be the most vulnerable, being subjected to high levels of stress when they are least experienced and probably more sleep deprived than at any time in their career. Even experienced general practitioners find night calls difficult, and these are a major reason for some wanting to retire early.

What is burnout?

Burnout is a condition that develops when an individual works too hard for too long in a high-pressure environment. The burnout victim is exhausted on all levels—physical, emotional and attitudinal. Burnout has no age limits; it can affect the idealistic trainee, hospital doctors, the struggling young general practitioner or even the senior partner.

Personalities of people at risk of burnout

Individuals who are most likely to develop burnout are those who are very productive and feel indispensable. They have high levels of energy, like to do a number of things at once, but do not know when to stop, have high expectations but are poor delegators. They are perfectionists and are addicted to setting themselves, and others, unrealistic targets at work and at play. They live with their foot constantly on the accelerator; they know where the brake is but they choose not to use it.

Overconscientious perfectionists with Type A personalities, those with so-called 'hurry sickness', are the most vulnerable. They are used to being in control and are the least likely to ask for help when things are beginning to go wrong. Type A people are highly competitive, unrelenting, hard driving and achievement orientated. They feel guilty or uneasy when relaxing or not working, and can be aggressive, hostile, restless and impatient, especially when unable rapidly to overcome obstacles to their own satisfaction.

Presentation and recognition of burnout

Burnout can be the result of mismanaged stress, especially if the warning signs have gone unrecognised. Health professionals and their patients can push themselves over the top of the human function curve, through fatigue and exhaustion, into ill-health, which is often a precursor of burnout.

Stress cannot be avoided. Human endeavour thrives on challenge and realistic ambitions; without it, boredom and apathy set in. The level of stress experienced depends not on the stressors themselves but on the way in which the individual reacts to them. The art is to live a full life with a minimum of wear and tear—to live more intelligently. Hans Selye, the founder of stress control, also observed that there is an optimum level of stress compatible with health, both mental and physical. Too much stress can result in disorderly thinking; in extreme form it leads to panic.

Zones of the human function curve

The human function curve can be divided into zones, with increased arousal leading eventually to burnout (Fig 1).

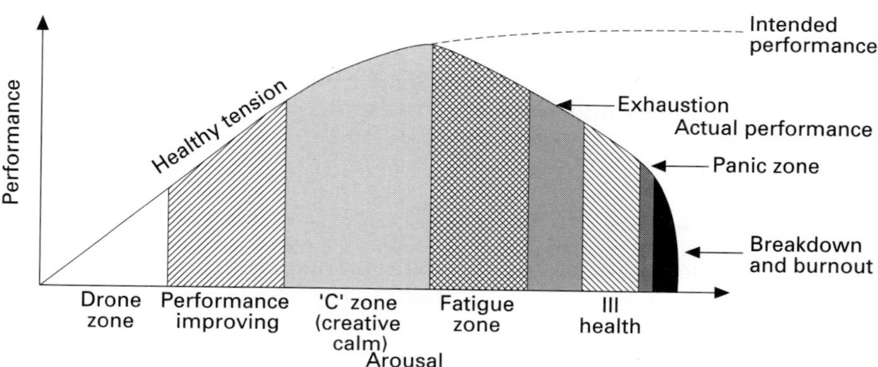

Fig 1. *Zones of the human function curve, from drone zone to burnout.*[1] With an increase in healthy tension, performance improves but at the top of the curve *fatigue,* if ignored, leads to a decline in performance. The *exhaustion* zone is followed by *ill-health.* At that point a small increase in pressure can cause *panic,* followed by *breakdown* and *burnout.*

Drone zone

The drone zone is at the bottom of the human function curve. It is characterised by insufficient challenge, too much mastery, and being uncommitted, overconfident, lethargic, sluggish and bored. There is low arousal and poor performance. The doctor in the drone zone may be in a branch of medicine to which he or she is unsuited, or he may even wish that he had not chosen medicine as a career.

Improving performance

Performance improves with increasing healthy tension. Idealism, hope and optimism are high. Stressors are being used intelligently to enhance performance and job satisfaction.

The 'C' zone

The 'C' zone is at the top of the human function curve; it is characterised by commitment, confidence, calm and being in control. Energised enthusiasm is associated with peak levels of performance.

Fatigue zone

The fatigue zone is just beyond the 'C' zone, over the top of the human function curve. Here performance is beginning to decline sharply as arousal continues to increase. Short-lived bouts of irritation are characteristic. Alcohol is frequently used for medicinal purposes to soothe jangled nerves. Caffeine may be abused to keep going and this can increase aggression. Sleep becomes more elusive with increasing tiredness; without rest, fatigue will lead to exhaustion.

Exhaustion zone

The exhaustion zone is where performance continues to decline. There is increasing anger and resentment, lasting for longer periods. Alcohol may be abused to combat chronic insomnia. Utter exhaustion is the enemy of health. There is neither virtue nor valour in driving ourselves until we are ill.

Ill-health zone

The ill-health zone is where the amber light is flashing a warning to take action. Any one of a number of physical disorders may have been provoked; these include ulcers, high blood pressure, angina, migraine, irritable bowel syndrome, asthma and diabetes. Becoming ill can be the price to pay for driving ourselves too hard.

Panic zone

The red light is flashing. The panic zone is where there is too much challenge, not enough mastery, things are now out of control and the victim feels 'hyper', scattered and nervous. Panic attacks may have started. A small amount of extra pressure can lead to breakdown and burnout.

Breakdown and burnout

The victim is struggling to keep going and urgently needs help. He is reluctant to go to work. Chronic insomnia and agitation have resulted in clinical depression, often with tearfulness and the risk of suicide. Road accidents and marital breakdown are common concomitants. Alcoholism or drug addiction may have become established.

This scheme is diagrammatic. There are not defined boundaries between the zones; many of us fluctuate between zones. At any stage before burnout, a break away from work, a holiday or a few good nights' sleep can restore equilibrium. However, the risk of burnout will return unless the potential victim changes his lifestyle.

Diagnosis of burnout

Self-diagnosis

Individuals may reflect upon whether they have symptoms which can indicate a vulnerability to burnout.

Physical symptoms:

- Fatigue
- Insomnia
- Headache
- Backache
- Gastrointestinal symptoms
- Weight loss/gain
- Shortness of breath
- Lingering cold

Personal symptoms:

- Depressed
- Chronically anxious
- Obsessed
- Feeling indispensable
- Restless
- Rationalising
- Stagnating
- Bored

Diagnosis of burnout in patients

The following symptoms are useful indications of burnout in patients:

- Emotional exhaustion with tiredness, somatic symptoms, irritability or outbursts of irrational anger, proneness to accidents, depression and tearfulness, excessive alcohol and caffeine consumption.
- Low productivity accompanied by feelings of low achievement, high absenteeism and a high sickness rate.
- Depersonalisation—treating individuals as if they are objects.

These symptoms are eloquently described by a manager from industry in the following passage:

> The 'old me' exhibited supreme confidence and knowledgeable experience, used to thrive under pressure and did the work of two men, taking short lunch hours and working a lot of overtime. Now I feel a sort of general nervousness, with a feeling that if anybody said or did something to upset me I would be likely to erupt like a seething volcano. I have a 'couldn't care less' attitude towards what other people might think of me and a deep desire to be left alone. My self-confidence has been shattered, and I no longer feel capable of handling anything that is thrown at me. I have lost interest and enthusiasm. I feel disillusion, resentment and despair. A great lethargy and depression, like a dark cloud, hangs over my head. I feel squeezed dry.

Burnout can have serious consequences for both the individual and the organisation, since those affected are often key personnel. Practitioners should therefore have a high level of suspicion so that the condition is recognised early and treatment, which is usually very effective, can be initiated.

Differential diagnosis of burnout

Conditions which may mimic burnout include:

- Somatic complaints that are not stress related.
- Clinical depression that is not precipitated by overwork.
- Alcoholism or drug addiction unrelated to work pressure.
- Phobic anxiety with panic attacks.

Post-traumatic stress disorder is not included in the differential diagnosis because it is characterised by an acute episode, followed by nightmares, insomnia and flashbacks, when the horrors of the trauma are relived. Burnout, by contrast, has an insidious onset and affects a personality type that ignores the warning signs of fatigue.

Complications of burnout

The complications of burnout are:

- Chronic fatigue
- Insomnia
- Ulcers
- Irritable bowel syndrome
- High blood pressure
- Angina
- Liability to heart attacks and strokes
- Migraine
- Poor work record and absenteeism
- Alcoholism
- Drug addiction
- Caffeinism
- Increased smoking
- Psychiatric illness, including clinical depression and chronic anxiety
- Asthma
- Diabetes
- Post-viral fatigue syndrome

Asthma and diabetes may be more difficult to control; the post-viral fatigue syndrome may be more likely to occur because of the body's reduced resistance to infections.

Alcohol problems

Alcohol is one of the first substances that people use to reduce stress; the second is caffeine to crank start the brain in the morning. Many will try to conceal their drink problem. A gamma GT (glutamyl transpeptidase) of greater than 40 IU/litre is found in about 80% of those with a drinking problem but many with advanced forms of the disease have normal liver function tests. A raised red cell mean corpuscular volume (MCV) of greater than 92 fl is found in about 60% of alcoholics. A blood alcohol determination can be very useful in workplaces that have an alcohol policy. Over 39 mg/100 ml impairs driving skills; 80 mg/100 ml is the legal limit for driving in Britain. A morning value above 150 mg/100 ml is likely to be diagnostic of alcoholism.

Urine alcohol concentrations exceeding 120 mg/100 ml are suggestive and over 200 mg/100 ml is diagnostic of alcoholism. The sample should be refrigerated and preferably frozen until analysis, otherwise false-positive results will be obtained, especially in diabetic patients, because of fermentation of glucose. Breath alcohol measurements reflect blood levels, are simple to perform and provide an immediate result. Breath alcometers can be used with a minimum of instruction. The smell of alcohol on the breath should alert the practitioner. I am always suspicious of patients with a moist handshake, smelling of peppermint.

Alcohol causes brain shrinkage seen on a computed tomography (CT) scan. Cognitive testing by a psychologist can be very useful in assessing intellectual damage, and determining whether judgement is likely to have been impaired. This is useful if a decision has to be made about an individual's continued ability to remain in post.

The CAGE questionnaire can be a good way of identifying those with a drinking problem. Two or more positive replies to the following four questions indicate a drinking problem with a 75% degree of accuracy.

- Have you ever felt you ought to cut down on your drinking?
- Have people annoyed you by criticising your drinking?
- Have you ever felt bad or guilty about your drinking?
- Have you ever had a drink first thing in the morning to steady your nerves or get rid of a hangover? ('eye-opener').

Treatment of burnout

Intake of alcohol and caffeine should be reduced or eliminated completely. Proper sleep should be restored if possible; this may be helped by a short course of temazepam at night, with a longer course of a sedative antidepressant, such as dothiepin (Prothiaden) or trimipramine (Surmontil), at night, or a serotonin reuptake inhibitor such as fluvoxamine (Faverin).

Lifestyle adjustment is facilitated by a break from work, a short holiday, and adoption of a regular exercise routine. Individuals must then address their work pattern to reduce stressors if rehabilitation is to be successful.

Stress reduction

The prevention of burnout is dependent upon the reduction of stress. The surgery or office, home and car should be as comfortable as possible. An active social life should be maintained, particularly one that involves other members of the family. In general practice, limiting the size of the list should also be considered. The job should be redesigned, allowing enough time for the unexpected by building in time buffer zones on a Monday or Friday—the days when more emergencies can be expected. The time allowed for a consultation should not be reduced to only 7 minutes, if it habitually takes 10 minutes. A spare consultation every three bookings will reduce the time pressure. It should be accepted that the unpredictable is part of being a general practitioner.

Poor management is one of the most common sources of stress in health professionals. Good management and a happy team will help everybody to cope with stress more efficiently. Time spent training, supporting and motivating the team will save a lot of wear and tear. For consultants in the NHS, the conflict of management demands versus patient care has been accentuated by the NHS reforms. General practitioners are overburdened by administrative demands.

More variety and 'time outs' should be provided at work.

Recreation and outdoor hobbies such as golf, fishing, sailing or tennis aid relaxation and free the individual from the shackles of the telephone. Portable telephones have advantages but they also increase stress by denying an individual private time and space.

Pets can be helpful. Their love and affection are not conditional on the triumphs and disasters of the day. During the first year after a heart attack, patients who do not own pets die at five times the rate of pet-owning patients.

Short breaks and a healthy lifestyle are better than taking long holidays, when pressure builds up before going away and there is often a mountain of correspondence to come back to.

Ten tips for coping with stress

1. Avoid self-medication with nicotine, too much alcohol, coffee or tranquillisers.
2. Work off stress by physical activity.
3. Do not put off relaxing; use a stress reduction technique daily, for example, transcendental meditation, yoga, progressive muscular relaxation, a relaxation cassette with or without biofeedback, autogenic training, autohypnosis, the Alexander technique or music.
4. Get enough sleep and rest to recharge your batteries; sleeping pills are unnecessary if your lifestyle can be changed.
5. If you become sick, do not try to carry on as if you are not.
6. Agree with somebody; life should not be a constant battle-ground; avoid entrenched interpersonal conflicts.
7. Learn to accept what you cannot change; to ignore this only leads to unhappiness, cynicism and bitterness.
8. Manage your time better and delegate; use a system that works for you, not against you; take one thing at a time and beware of overdoing Type A behaviour; create time buffers to deal with unexpected emergencies.
9. Know when you are tired and do something about it; it is difficult to go to sleep when feeling either anxious or angry.
10. Plan ahead; by saying 'No' now you may prevent too much pressure building up in the future.

Prevention of professional burnout

Burnout has an insidious onset and usually starts with workaholism and preoccupation with time. Initially it affects work quality and later all aspects of life. It is not the same as depression and it is easier to prevent than to treat. It requires good communication and watchfulness of the team. It can be prevented by tender loving care and rationing of workload.

The 'Ten tips for coping with stress' should be used regularly, with a relaxation technique (the third of the ten tips). No single method works for everybody, and individuals will persist with their method of choice only if they obtain benefit from it. Change is always difficult, and developing a new lifestyle with time for regular relaxation demands considerable willpower.

Use a relaxation technique daily

Research has shown that transcendental meditation (TM) for 20 minutes twice a day has a marked beneficial impact on health. It recharges the flagging brain, lowers blood pressure, heart rate and cholesterol. There is a diminished use of alcohol, cigarettes and less anxiety and insomnia. In a controlled study,[2] hospital admissions for transcendental meditators were reduced by 50%, and there was an 87% reduction in admissions for heart disease and diseases of the nervous system. Admissions for benign and malignant tumours were reduced by 55%, and those for mental disorders and infectious diseases by 30%. This study was conducted with an American insurance company on 2,000 meditators, who were compared with the 600,000 member database of the same insurance carrier. Insurance companies in the USA now offer a discount on their premiums to patients who meditate because they are convinced of their superior health record. In The Netherlands, the largest health insurance company, Silver Cross, offers a 30% discount to all transcendental meditators.

In a recent Canadian controlled study,[3] it was found that in Quebec health costs of TM practitioners declined 12.4% annually. Over the 3 year period since learning TM, the cumulative change was approximately 36%.

Reduction in alcohol intake

Alcohol consumption should be no more than 21 units of alcohol per week, with two alcohol-free days, for men, and 14 units a week for women. The General Medical Council classified 37% of general practitioners whom they investigated as alcoholics or drug addicts.

Reduction of caffeine intake

Coffee has a long half-life (6 hours). It can therefore accumulate in the blood and brain throughout the day and cause insomnia, anxiety, restlessness, nervousness, irritability, agitation, depression, palpitations and headaches. These symptoms can be produced in some patients by no more than 150 mg of caffeine per day (approximately two cups of coffee). Tea, Coca-Cola and Diet Coke also contain caffeine; decaffeinated Coke is available.

Increased exercise

Exercise can be a useful destressor. It reduces the level of adrenaline released by pressure or anger, produces 'good mood' agents (endorphins) in the brain, and leads to a sense of wellbeing and relaxation. Some writers use the elevation of mood after exercise to do their most creative work. However, some people feel ill if they exercise and it is possible that their brain endorphin production is in some way different.

Prognosis of burnout

If burnout is recognised and treated early, the prognosis is excellent. If left to gather momentum, a psychiatric referral may become necessary, and there is a risk that burnout, as the name implies, can become permanent. Such victims never return to their high premorbid levels of performance or even to their profession. Some take early retirement and others have early retirement or redundancy thrust upon them.

Conclusion

Burnout is not uncommon in medicine and indeed the term was originally applied to carers though it also affects other highly stressed professions, such as dentistry, teaching and the police. Being aware of and looking for warning signs is not difficult. Health carers who work too hard for too long place their patients at risk.

We can decide to spend our life on the treadmill of medicine, getting more and more exhausted. The alternative is to use the 'ten tips' to our advantage. I have prepared a leaflet[4] to help people stay on a healthy 'medicine wheel', instead of a treadmill. We could learn from the Spiritual Teaching of a Cheyenne Indian: 'Any idea, person or object can make a Medicine Wheel, a mirror for man. The tiniest flower can be such a mirror, as can a dog [wolf in the original quote], a story, a touch, a religion or a mountain top'.

It is not what you know but what you do with what you know that counts. Take care of yourself; with better balance and good health you can have happiness and freedom from disease.

References

1. Kelly D. Professional burnout. *Update* 1992; **44:** 1163–70
2. Orme-Johnson D. Medical care utilization and the Transcendental Meditation Programme. *Psychosomatic Medicine* 1987; **49**: 493–507
3. Herron RE. The impact of Transcendental Meditation practice on medical expenditures. *Dissertation Abstracts International.* Issue 12; Book A; Volume 53 1993, pp 1–14
4. Kelly D. *Taking the strain out of stress.* Priory Hospitals Group, 1994 (Available from the author)

7 Depression and suicide in doctors and medical students

David S Baldwin
Senior Lecturer, Faculty of Medicine, University of Southampton; Consultant in General and Community Psychiatry, Royal South Hants Hospital, Southampton
Shauna E Rudge
Senior Registrar in Psychiatry, Charing Cross Hospital, London

---

In January 1992 the Defeat Depression campaign was launched with the aims of increasing the knowledge of health care professionals in the recognition and effective management of depressive illness, and enhancing public awareness of the nature, course and treatment of depression.[1] Since it is clear that doctors are not especially adept at recognising depression in their patients,[2] it seems reasonable to assume that similar problems exist in acknowledging the presence of depression in themselves, or in identifying it in their colleagues. This chapter provides an overview of the literature on depression and suicide in doctors and medical students, before proceeding to argue that the public messages of the campaign are as relevant to doctors as to other members of the general population.

Suicide—a reflection of increased rates of depression in doctors?

Surprisingly little is known of the true prevalence of depression in doctors. The limited findings of the research which has been performed tend to suggest that medical practitioners may be at increased risk of suicide, and also indicate that medical students and junior doctors report high levels of emotional distress.

Mortality is a widely used measure of overall health in epidemiological studies. For the purposes of this review, it seems reasonable to regard deaths from suicide, accidents, and from liver disease with cirrhosis as being a reflection of overall mental health at the time of death. In the United Kingdom, reports on occupational mortality are produced after each Office of Population Censuses and Surveys (OPCS) national census, utilising information derived from the census and from death certificates. The standardised mortality ratio (SMR) for subjects in differing occupations can then be calculated, by comparing the number of deaths which have occurred with those which would have been expected if the group in question had the same age-specific mortality as the general population. SMRs can be calculated both for overall mortality and for those deaths due to specific diseases or conditions.

The 1986 decennial supplement on occupational mortality links deaths during the periods 1979–80 and 1982–83 with data from the 1981 census.[3] For male medical practitioners, overall and most disease-specific mortality ratios tend to be less than those for the general population (Table 1). However, there is some evidence of an increased risk of death from chronic liver disease and cirrhosis, external injury and poisoning, and suicide. The same general patterns can be seen in female doctors. Women *appear* to be at an even greater risk of suicide, the SMR for fatal self-harm notably exceeding that of their male counterparts. However, the absolute number of deaths from suicide in women is much lower, such that the difference in SMR from the general population fails to reach the traditional levels of statistical significance (Table 1).

The OPCS figures on suicide are generally supported by the findings of other forms of research.[4] Most investigations indicate that medical practitioners have a rate of suicide that is at least double that of the rest of the population. However, it should be remembered that suicide is perhaps generally more common in social class I, and that increased risks of self-harm appear to apply not only to doctors but also to all workers within the health service.[5] Among medical practitioners, female doctors[6,7] and those who have recently qualified[8,9] may be at increased risk. Certain medical specialties appear to be particularly associated with high

Table 1. Mortality of the medical profession (SMR for all causes and certain specific causes of death)[3]

	Men	Women
All causes	66*	79
Chronic liver disease	115	—
Injury and poisoning	182†	182*
Suicide	172*	371

Data refer to men aged 20–64 years and single women aged 16–60 years.

* Statistically different from 100 at 95% confidence interval.

† Statistically different from 100 at 99% confidence interval.

rates of suicide; these include anaesthetics,[10] pathology,[11,12] psychiatry[13] and radiology.[14]

Although it is difficult to identify those who are at risk of self-harm with great accuracy, it has been argued that suicide is a consequence of depression, for which a range of effective treatments is available, and that suicide therefore represents a preventable cause of death.[15] Suicide among doctors has been reported to be associated with a history of depression, the presence of physical or other forms of mental illness, problem drinking, the use of self-prescribed medication, and poor social support.[4] Research is needed to clarify whether the identification of such problems, with appropriate intervention, could result in the prevention of suicide in doctors.

Emotional distress—a marker of depression in doctors?

Morbidity is generally considered to be a more satisfactory measure of overall health than mortality. Clearly, many causes of serious ill-health result in death only rarely. However, the measurement of morbidity is rather more complex, and is usually dependent upon the use of surrogate variables which indicate the presence or absence of illness and the severity of disease. Measurement of lung function, for example, may allow the identification of pulmonary disease. Unfortunately, problems abound in the realm of mental health, where it may be especially difficult to define the boundaries between health and illness. Nevertheless, 'markers' of overall emotional distress are frequently used in epidemiological research, typically with the aim of identifying 'cases' of psychological disorder. The General Health Questionnaire (GHQ),[16] for example, has been utilised in a series of investigations of the mental health of medical students and junior hospital doctors in the United Kingdom.[17–19]

During the pre-registration year, it was found that 50% of house officers reported significant degrees of emotional distress, most of this group describing depressive symptoms of a severity similar to that seen in depressive illness.[18] Female doctors were particularly likely to report significant psychological distress—indeed, some 50% of female house officers were markedly troubled by depressive symptoms.[19] Findings such as these are replicated by the results of other studies conducted outside the British Isles. In two North American investigations, for example, it was found that approximately 40% of interns fulfilled the diagnostic criteria for a major depressive episode, this again being especially likely in female doctors.[20,21]

There have been few systematic investigations of the mental health of general practitioners (GPs). Two postal surveys performed in the UK suggest that GPs are adapting rather poorly to recent changes in the organisation of the National Health Service. Prior to the reforms, female GPs would appear to have enjoyed remarkably good mental health, reporting less anxiety, depression and 'stress' than a normative UK population. By contrast, male GPs reported more anxiety, although their scores for depression and 'stress' were not significantly different from those seen in the reference group.[22] However, in the second survey, which was conducted after the major reorganisation of the NHS, GPs as a whole reported more 'stress', less job satisfaction, and poorer overall mental health than that described at the time of the first survey.[23]

The results of a third survey, of GPs, hospital consultants and health service managers,[24] also indicate that senior doctors and managers report high levels of stress, anxiety and depression. When completing the GHQ,[16] 47% of the total sample reported high levels of emotional distress, there being no differences within the three sub-groups. However, scores on the self-report Hospital Anxiety and Depression Scale[25] indicated significant degrees of anxiety in 30% of the GPs and managers, and in 23% of the hospital consultants. Significant levels of depression were found in 11% of GPs and in 5% of the consultants, but in none of the group of 67 managers—a somewhat unusual finding.

Unfortunately the results of the first two of these surveys are unreliable as large numbers of those questioned failed to return their replies. Regrettably, much of the research in this area has been rather limited in design, so it is still not possible to attribute causal roles to particular aspects of a doctor's work. Although a recent review of the literature on the health of junior doctors reasonably stated that 'it is difficult to escape the conclusion that certain aspects of a junior doctor's job appear to be contributing to a high incidence of mental health problems',[26] it is hard to establish with any accuracy exactly which aspects are proving detrimental. It remains unclear whether problems may arise simply because of the long hours of work of many doctors, or whether the emotionally charged content of much of the job is of more importance.[27] Furthermore, it is most unlikely that the medical profession constitutes a homogeneous group with regard to either psychological resilience or the vulnerability to 'stress'. Differences in age, gender and chosen specialty may render particular individuals especially prone to emotional distress when faced with particular types of adverse experience.

Mental health problems in medical students

Many students are subject to the pressures of information overload, examinations and financial difficulties. It has been argued that the stresses on medical students are greater than those on other undergraduates, simply because the typical medical school curriculum is lengthier, broader and more detailed than most other forms of university education.[28] Although the format of the course undoubtedly confers additional stress, much must also arise from the unique content of the undergraduate years; from an early stage, for example, medical students are required to master interview and clinical skills, to gain experience of trauma, surgery and mental illness, and to cope with the disease and death of patients with whom they may have developed emotional attachments. These requirements may be associated with the development of quite marked emotional distress, and it therefore seems understandable that the mental health of medical students has been subject to a range of investigations.[17,29,30]

Although the results of these studies are rather varied, it would appear that medical students tend to be more emotionally troubled than other groups, and that they may be suffering from greater degrees of stress than that experienced by students of other subjects.[29] One study, for example, found that around 15–35% of medical students were suffering from some form of psychiatric morbidity.[30] Researchers have attempted to identify the personal characteristics of those students who are considered to be at greatest risk of emotional distress, as this could be of some relevance to the initial interview for entry into medical school. These attempts have proved largely unsuccessful, with most studies providing little evidence for the delineation of the personality traits and other qualities that will eventually lead to a good doctor.[4]

It has been suggested that the medical profession resorts to the abuse of alcohol in a misguided attempt to deal with the high levels of stress in everyday clinical work.[4] Maladaptive patterns of drinking may become established early in a medical career, but should be reasonably amenable to intervention once the problem is recognised and if appropriate advice is available. Given the popular interest in the consumption of alcohol by medical students, it seems surprising that this has been investigated in only a limited number of studies.[17,31–33] Before considering the results of these investigations, it should be remembered that students as an overall group may tend to drink more heavily than other adults of the same age, and it is possible that the drinking behaviour of medical undergraduates is determined by their membership of the body of students, rather than being a reflection of their intended career.[31]

However, the limited evidence which is available does indeed suggest that medical students consume alcohol to an excessive degree. In an early investigation, approximately 20% of medical students at three British universities admitted to drinking heavily, and 48% of the students reported an increase in their alcohol intake over the 2 years prior to the study.[31] In a further investigation of a sample of British medical students, the mean consumption of alcohol was found to be approximately 20 units per week in males and around 12 units per week in females.[32] Nearly a quarter of the students exceeded 'safe' levels of drinking, and over half of the subjects admitted that their academic performance had been impaired by alcohol at some time. The pattern of drinking amongst male students was similar to that reported by the male population of the same age. Female medical students, however, drank more alcohol than other females of the same age. The linkage between measures of academic performance and levels of drinking is far from established, however, as the results of a more recent investigation failed to reveal any relationship.[33]

Prevalence of depression in doctors

Depression is a surprisingly common disorder. Although estimates vary, it seems that approximately 50% of women and 25% of men will suffer from a depressive disorder at some time during their lives.[34] Community surveys of the general population indicate that around 3–6% of adults are suffering from depression at any one time.[1] Although the course of depression in primary care settings is not fully established, it is known that the majority of patients will experience an episodic recurring illness.[35]

The prevalence of depression within the medical profession is unknown. Typically, working populations are expected to be more healthy than the general population, as ill people are less likely to find and maintain employment. It is noteworthy that surrogate 'markers' of mental disorder, such as the presence of high levels of emotional distress in some surveys, or the finding of increased rates of suicide in occupational mortality statistics, suggest that doctors are at great risk of depression. The seemingly high level of emotional distress in doctors should be the cause of some concern, particularly when the nature of clinical work is considered. There is a clear need for more detailed research, so that the true prevalence of mental disorder within the medical profession can be established with greater accuracy.

Epidemiological investigations of the prevalence of depression in doctors would need to employ a two-stage design. Possible 'cases' of emotional disorder might be identified through the use of conventional screening instruments such as the GHQ.[16] Those who appear to be psychologically troubled could then be examined using standardised clinical interview schedules that utilise generally accepted diagnostic criteria, for example those specified within the tenth edition of the International Classification of Diseases (Table 2).

It is perhaps unfortunate that terms such as 'stress' and 'burnout' are utilised so frequently when describing the psychological difficulties of health care professionals. Although the use of these terms may focus attention on the problem of emotional distress in doctors in an acceptable fashion, it is possible that recording a user-friendly diagnosis could result in the failure to recognise serious underlying mental disorders, such as depressive illness. For example, the commoner features of 'stress' appear to be virtually indistinguishable from the symptoms and signs of psychological and somatic anxiety. Similarly, the cardinal features of 'burnout' are said to include tiredness, low mood, irritability, reduced productivity and feelings of low achievement, all of which are well recognised features of depression.

Furthermore, the use of 'burnout' not only implies that the problems of an employee have mainly arisen in the workplace but also suggests that their solution lies either within altering the

Table 2. Depressive episode; diagnostic criteria (criteria for ICD-10 depressive episode)

Typical symptoms	Depressed mood
	Loss of interest and enjoyment
	Reduced energy
Other symptoms	Reduced concentration and attention
	Reduced self-esteem and self-confidence
	Ideas of guilt and worthlessness
	Bleak and pessimistic views of the future
	Ideas or acts of self-harm or suicide
	Disturbed sleep
	Diminished appetite

Source: *The ICD-10 Classification of Mental and Behavioural Disorders.* World Health Organization (1992).

attitude to work and the way in which it is performed or by making changes in the working environment. Such approaches will fail to address the problems of those who have become troubled for reasons other than problems at work. By contrast, the term 'depression' merely signifies a recognisable constellation of symptoms and signs, without making any assumptions regarding a presumed aetiology. Treatment is then determined by the degree of personal distress and the severity of the clinical syndrome.

Consequences of depression in doctors

Depression is a particularly malignant and disabling disorder. It is known to be associated with increased morbidity and mortality from a variety of physical disorders, and has its own mortality through accidents, neglect and suicide.[36] Unfortunately the social consequences of depression are often overlooked. It can interfere with personal and marital relationships, contributes to family discord, and may prejudice the development of children. Furthermore, depression significantly reduces the capacity for work, and may have adverse effects on financial income. The economic burden of depression to society is enormous but has only recently become the subject of attention.[37]

Regrettably, depressive illness in doctors can result in additional problems, extending far beyond the immediate circle of family and friends. Patients may suffer unnecessarily, colleagues can be inconvenienced, and the place of work disadvantaged. For example, the loss of drive and the easier fatigue of depression may reduce the quantity of clinical work which could otherwise have been performed. Brooding and withdrawal may affect the quality of care that is provided; increased irritability may result in frustration and intolerance, and might lead to a less sympathetic approach to patients and their relatives. Rarely, the undue pessimism and impaired judgement of severe depression may lead to therapeutic nihilism or even to dangerous mistakes. Others suffer too. The excessive worrying and pathological indecisiveness so characteristic of depression can interfere with the ability to lead a team effectively. The capacity to supervise and train junior medical staff may be reduced. Sickness absence will impose additional burdens upon colleagues struggling to maintain the usual service. Finally, the reduced productivity of depression can lead to a substantial loss in financial revenue for the employing authority.[37]

Prevention of depression in doctors

In common with most other forms of mental disorder, depressive illness is presumed to have a multifactorial aetiology. It seems likely that the prevention of depression in doctors will therefore require a multifaceted approach including, for example, changes in undergraduate medical education and postgraduate training, and alterations to the structure and function of occupational health services (see Table 3).

By convention, preventive measures are described as being either primary, secondary or tertiary in nature. Primary prevention is aimed at reducing the incidence of disease. Unfortunately no aetiological model of depression is sufficiently robust to allow the development of specific interventions which would eliminate the factors that cause or contribute to the onset of depression. However, it is possible to believe that changes to the education, training and work of doctors may produce beneficial effects in reducing the seemingly high levels of emotional distress. Nevertheless, the most important initiatives in a 'health promotion package' for preventing depression in doctors are likely to be in the realm of secondary and tertiary prevention.

Secondary prevention aims to reduce the prevalence of disease, through early detection and prompt and effective intervention. It would embrace all those efforts which encourage the prompt recognition of depressed individuals, perhaps through opportunistic screening at pre-employment checks of health status. Tertiary prevention of depression seeks to minimise the consequences and complications of the disorder once it has been diagnosed. Unfortunately, secondary prevention of depression in doctors is

Table 3. Prevention of mental disorder (requires changes in many aspects of current practice)[28]

- Undergraduate medical education
- Careers advice
- Postgraduate training
- Management training
- Manpower
- Working hours
- General facilities
- Mental health policies
- Counselling
- Occupational health

hindered by the behaviour of the medical profession itself. Doctors are often reluctant to discuss their emotional problems, perhaps because of concerns relating to loss of face or to career progress. Self-diagnosis and self-prescribing still abound, with potentially damaging consequences. Furthermore, there is a tendency for overt mental health problems in colleagues to be ignored until such time as mistakes in clinical management become ever more conspicuous.

For a profession that is concerned with health, it seems rather ironic that the health facilities for doctors are so often under-used or inadequate. Many doctors fail to register with a local GP, and occupational health services within the NHS may be the poorest in the country.[38] Action is required to improve the standing of occupational health services, and to raise the awareness of the need for such provisions for all staff working within the NHS.

Conclusions

Although this chapter has sought to focus attention on the mental health problems of medical practitioners, much of the content is of relevance to other workers within the National Health Service. Attempts to resolve the problem of depression in doctors may require a variety of specific efforts, such as changes to the undergraduate curriculum[39] and to the patterns of postgraduate training.[40] However, further help could be provided by the introduction of changes which may have a rather more general application to all NHS employees.

Every hospital or Family Health Services Authority (FHSA) should give consideration to the development of a 'mental health policy'. Such a policy should not only aim to encourage the prompt recognition and effective treatment of depressed employees but also attempt to facilitate a working environment which is conducive to the prevention of depression and other forms of mental illness. These management initiatives would be expected to improve the contribution of individual employees, should reduce the costs incurred by sickness absence due to depression and many physical disorders, and could enhance the overall performance of the hospital trust or FHSA.[37]

Clearly, the exact form of such a programme will be dependent upon local needs and resources. Suggestions regarding the development of a mental health policy can be found in a booklet[37] and an educational package for personnel and occupational health departments,[41] both entitled *Depression in the workplace* and produced by the Defeat Depression campaign. Typically, a mental health policy might choose to concentrate on four main areas.

Raising awareness of depression

Everyone in the organisation, including senior management, must be made aware of the importance of recognising and helping colleagues who may be suffering from depression. It is fundamental that everyone should understand that positive action can result in great benefits to individuals and to the service that is provided.

Health education for employees

Employees should benefit from a greater knowledge of mental health issues, and from further education regarding the specific techniques for reducing stress and anxiety. Instruction in time-management skills and assertiveness training may be particularly appropriate.

Organisation of the business

Both the structure and the function of an organisation are likely to exert an effect on the mental health of its workforce. Important areas include the physical environment at work, the responsibilities inherent in the job, the level of supervision that is available, and the selection and training of personnel for particular tasks. Thoughtful adjustments to organisational structure can enhance the job satisfaction of individual employees and the performance of the business.

Occupational health services

Occupational health departments should be involved in the development of programmes which attempt to educate managers and the workforce in the prevention, recognition and treatment of depression. Occupational health services should also have a special role in the recognition, counselling and treatment of depressed employees, and in facilitating their return to work.

Acknowledgements

The authors wish to thank Mary Pascal of West London Healthcare NHS Trust for secretarial support and Paul Valentine of the

Coombs Library for help with the literature search. Much of the content of the literature review was obtained from two excellent books published by the British Medical Association.[4,28] Copies of the booklet and package *Depression in the workplace* are available from the Royal College of Psychiatrists.

References

1. Paykel ES, Priest RG. Recognition and management of depression in general practice: consensus statement. *British Medical Journal* 1992; **305**: 1198–202
2. Tylee AT, Freeling P. The recognition, diagnosis and acknowledgement of depressive disorder by general practitioners. In: Herbst K, Paykel E (eds). *Depression: an integrative approach.* Oxford: Heinemann, 1988: 216–31
3. OPCS. *Occupational mortality 1979–1980, 1982–1983.* London: HMSO, 1986
4. British Medical Association. *The morbidity and mortality of the medical profession.* London: BMA, 1993
5. Balarajan R. Inequalities in health within the health sector. *British Medical Journal* 1989; **229**: 822–5
6. Harrington JM, Oakes D. Mortality study of British pathologists 1974–1980. *British Journal of Industrial Medicine* 1984; **41**: 188–91
7. Schlicht SM, Gordon IR, Ball JRB, Christie DGS. Suicide and related deaths in Victorian doctors. *Medical Journal of Australia* 1990; **153**: 518–21
8. King H. Health in the medical and other learned professions. *Journal of Chronic Diseases* 1970; **23**: 257–81
9. Anonymous. Mortality of anaesthesiologists. *Statistical Bulletin of the Metropolitan Life Insurance Company* 1974; **55**: 5–8
10. Lew EA. Mortality experience among anaesthesiologists, 1954–1976. *Anaesthesiology* 1979; **51**: 195–9
11. Harrington JM, Shannon HS. Mortality study of pathologists and medical laboratory technicians. *British Medical Journal* 1975; **i**: 329–32
12. Hall A, Harrington JM, Aw TC. Mortality study of British pathologists. *American Journal of Industrial Medicine* 1991; **20**: 83–9
13. Rich CL, Pitts FN. Suicide by psychiatrists: a study of medical specialists among 18,730 consecutive physician deaths during a five-year period, 1967–1972. *Journal of Clinical Psychiatry* 1980; **41**: 262–3
14. Matanoski GM, Seltser R, Sartwell PE, Diamond EL, Elliott EA. The current mortality rates of radiologists and other physician specialists: specific causes of death. *American Journal of Epidemiology* 1975; **101**: 199–210
15. Secretary of State for Health. *The health of the nation: a strategy for health in England.* London: HMSO, 1992
16. Goldberg DP. *Manual of the General Health Questionnaire.* Windsor: NFER, 1978
17. Firth J. Levels and sources of stress in medical students. *British Medical Journal* 1986; **292**: 1177–80

18. Firth-Cozens J. Emotional distress in junior house officers. *British Medical Journal* 1987; **295**: 533–6
19. Firth-Cozens J. Sources of stress in women junior house officers. *British Medical Journal* 1990; **301**: 89–91
20. Butterfield PS. The stress of residency: a review of the literature. *Archives of Internal Medicine* 1988; **148**: 1428–35
21. Hsu K, Marshall V. Prevalence of depression and distress in a large sample of Canadian residents, interns and fellows. *American Journal of Psychiatry* 1987; **144**: 1561–6
22. Cooper CL, Rout U, Faragher B. Mental health, job satisfaction and job stress among general practitioners. *British Medical Journal* 1989; **298**: 366–70
23. Sutherland VJ, Cooper CL. Job stress, satisfaction and mental health among general practitioners before and after introduction of new contract. *British Medical Journal* 1992; **304**: 1545–8
24. Caplan RP. Stress, anxiety and depression in hospital consultants, general practitioners, and senior health service managers. *British Medical Journal* 1994; **309**: 1261–3
25. Zigmond AS, Snaith RP. The hospital anxiety and depression scale. *Acta Psychiatrica Scandinavica* 1983; **67**: 361–70
26. Spurgeon A, Harrington JM. Work performance and health of junior hospital doctors—a review of the literature. *Work and Stress* 1989; **3**: 117–28
27. Harrington JM. Working long hours and health. *British Medical Journal* 1994; **308**: 1581–2
28. British Medical Association. *Stress and the medical profession.* London: BMA, 1992
29. Payne R, Firth-Cozens J. *Stress in health professionals.* Chichester: John Wiley, 1987
30. Firth-Cozens J. Stress in medical undergraduates and house officers. *British Journal of Hospital Medicine* 1989; **41**: 161–4
31. Anderson P. Alcohol consumption of undergraduates at Oxford University. *Alcohol and Alcoholism* 1984; **19**: 77–84
32. Collier DJ, Beales ILP. Drinking among medical students: a questionnaire survey. *British Medical Journal* 1989; **299**: 19–22
33. File SE, Mabbutt PS, Shaffer J. Alcohol consumption and lifestyle in medical students. *Journal of Psychopharmacology* 1994; **8**: 22–6
34. Hagnell O, Lanke J, Rorsman B, Ojeslo L. Are we entering an age of melancholy? Depressive illnesses in a prospective epidemiological study over 25 years: the Lundby study, Sweden. *Psychological Medicine* 1982; **12**: 279–85
35. Angst J. How recurrent and predictable is depressive illness? In: Montgomery SA, Rouillon R (eds). *Long term treatment of depression.* Perspectives in Psychiatry, Volume 3. Chichester: John Wiley, 1992
36. Guze SB, Robins E. Suicide and primary affective disorders. *British Journal of Psychiatry* 1970; **117**: 437–8
37. Baldwin DS, Merson SR. *Depression in the workplace.* Defeat Depression campaign booklet produced by the Royal College of Psychiatrists, 1993
38. British Medical Association. *Leading for health: a BMA agenda for health.* London: BMA, 1991

39. General Medical Council. *Tomorrow's doctors: recommendations on undergraduate medical education.* London: GMC, 1993
40. Department of Health. *Hospital doctors: training for the future.* London: HMSO, 1993
41. Defeat Depression Campaign. *Depression in the workplace: an educational package for employers.* London, 1995

8 Occupational stress in health care workers

David W Rees
Director of Psychology Services,
North Manchester Healthcare (NHS) Trust

This chapter examines the problems of occupational stress amongst health care workers. It begins with a look at some of the organisational costs of stress, it considers the various ways in which the concept of stress has been used, it seeks some of the more important causes of stress and this leads on to a presentation of the results of a stress audit conducted in a directly managed unit 'Darkshire'.

Organisational costs of stress

It has been estimated that stress-related illnesses are responsible for more absenteeism from work than any other single cause. There are many estimates of the cost of stress. For example, it has been estimated that in 1992 sickness absence cost UK employers over £13 billion and that some 40% of this was stress-related. Other estimates suggest that 30 million working days are lost each year because of stress.

The NHS is the largest employer in the UK. It has been suggested that the NHS loses the equivalent of 10,000 whole time equivalent (w.t.e.) staff through medically certified sickness each year, and of these staff 4,000 w.t.e. are lost because of stress. Sickness absence is not the only consequence that can be costed. The cost of accidents to the NHS has been estimated as being as high as 5% of annual turnover. A recent survey[1] found that nearly a third of health service staff were on some kind of medication linked to stress. They were also likely to turn to alcohol and cigarettes as a way of coping with pressures at work. It was estimated that 83% of staff suffered from some degree of stress.

Health workers are particularly susceptible to developing stress-related illness because of the nature of their work.[2] Health professionals face occupational stressors which are not a feature of most other occupations and routinely deal with people in situations which have profound implications, often involving death and suffering. It has been suggested that a government health warning should be imprinted in every health professional's mind: 'Caring can damage your health'.[3] The term 'burnout' has been coined to describe the effects of the kinds of stress experienced by some health professionals.

These estimates of the costs of stress are on a scale which may be difficult to comprehend. The data presented later, which are taken from a stress audit carried out in a directly managed unit, may be more comprehensible to those concerned with the NHS and other organisations.

What is stress?

The word 'stress' is used in a number of ways in the literature and this can be confusing and misleading for the reader. We need to distinguish between stress that refers to environmental demands and pressures which we may perceive as either good (because we are able to cope) or bad (unable to cope) and stress that refers to the consequences of the external demands.[4] Thus stress is used as an external challenge (which can be positive), as an external hardship (which when intolerable is negative) and as an individual's reaction to stress.

Figure 1 shows diagrammatically the relationship between pressure (as an external demand) and performance. As the diagram shows, a certain amount of pressure is required to reach an optimum level of performance. If the pressure is too low the

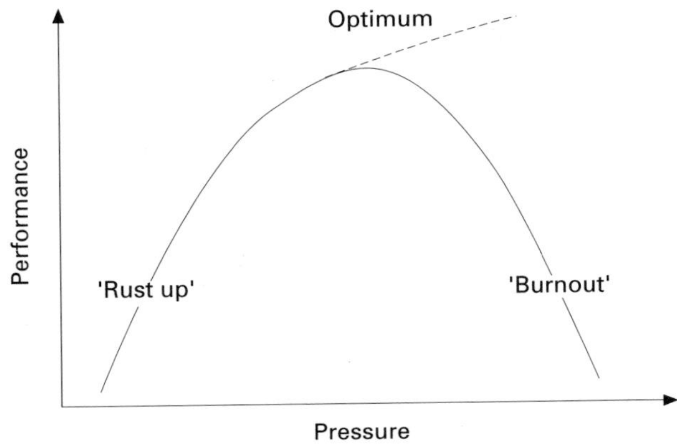

Fig 1. *The relationship between pressure and performance*

individual may experience the stress of 'rust up' in which there is monotony and boredom. However, once the optimum level of performance is achieved, additional pressure will serve to impinge on performance and will ultimately result in burnout. This is an important relationship because there is a widespread misconception that the application of more and more pressure will cause performance to continue to rise beyond the optimum, as shown by a broken line in the diagram.

A number of attempts have been made to identify the employment characteristics which have a strong influence on stress levels. One of the most influential of these studies has been reported by Warr[5] who identified nine key job characteristics:

1. Low job discretion
2. Low use of skills
3. Low or high work demands
4. Low task variety
5. High uncertainty
6. Low pay
7. Poor working conditions
8. Low interpersonal support
9. Low value in society

Warr discusses each characteristic in turn; his analysis will not be repeated here. However, it is important to recognise that these nine characteristics are each the end of a continuous variable and that all jobs can be analysed in this way. Analysing one's own post and those of colleagues and patients can be revealing.

A stress audit of a directly managed NHS unit 'Darkshire'

Cary Cooper, the UK's leading authority on occupational stress, believes that every organisation should carry out its own stress audit. This needs to be done before rushing to introduce measures such as time management, counselling or relaxation courses. Organisations should identify their own problems and assess whether they should redesign jobs, introduce greater flexibility or change traditional career paths as a way of improving employee well-being.

The following results are taken from a stress audit[6] carried out in one directly managed unit, called 'Darkshire', in the north west region of England.

Darkshire

Darkshire provides hospital and community services to a resident population of 135,000 people and to a catchment population of 200,000. Two-thirds of the district is designated as 'inner city' and it is one of the most socially deprived areas in England with very high levels of morbidity. At the time of the study Darkshire had approximately 4,400 employees working in a district general hospital, three peripheral hospitals and a range of community settings.

Subjects

A disproportionate stratified sample of staff was identified to ensure adequate representation of all occupational groups by grade, shift worked, and full-time or part-time status. This was done by taking the names of all employees from the Integrated Personnel System and choosing each cluster at random. Staff who were on either long-term sick or maternity leave were excluded from the study.

A total of 1,754 questionnaires were distributed to potential respondents and 1,176 were returned for analysis, a response rate of 67%. Table 1 shows the numbers and proportions of staff in each occupational group who returned completed questionnaires. Of the total sample, 72% were female, 88% worked regular days, 6% nights and 84% worked full-time.

Table 1. Stress audit respondents

	Number	%
Administrative and clerical staff	129	69
Ancillary staff	65	39
Doctors—Juniors	97	57
Consultants	56	60
Nurses	555	68
PAMs (professions allied to medicine)*	147	75
Scientists and technicians	66	57
General managers	12	80
Occupation not known	49	
	1,176	67

*Occupational therapists, physiotherapists, dietitians, speech therapists.

Measures and procedure

The identified study sample of staff were sent the Occupational Stress Indicator,[7] a questionnaire which asked about a number of socio-demographic and job-related variables; in addition subjects were asked to state how many days sick leave they had taken in the previous 6 months.

The Occupational Stress Indicator

The Occupational Stress Indicator (OSI) is an instrument designed to assess a number of stress elements which are mediated by a range of sources of individual differences (type A behaviour pattern; perceived locus of control; use of coping strategies) to result in a number of strain effects (current state of health; job satisfaction). The structure of the model assessed by the OSI is shown in Table 2. A description of the OSI and its elements can be found in Rees and Cooper.[6] The OSI has been widely used in the UK, particularly in stress audits of organisations, with the result that the normative data available on the instrument are extensive and include norms based on more than 3,000 health care workers.

Table 2. Structure of the Occupational Stress Indicator

Stress elements	Individual differences	Strain effects
Sources of pressure	*Type A behaviour pattern*	*Current state of health*
Intrinsic to the job	Attitude to living	Mental ill-health
Management role	Style of behaviour	Physical ill-health
Relationships with others	Ambition	
Career and achievement		*Job satisfaction*
Organisational structure and climate	*Perceived locus of control*	Achievement, value and growth
Home/work interface	Organisational forces	Job itself
	Management process	Organisational design
	Individual influence	Organisational processes
		Personal
	Use of coping strategies	Relationships
	Social support	
	Task strategies	
	Logic	
	Home/work relations	
	Time management	
	Involvement	

Briefly, the OSI looks at six categories of sources of pressure in the workplace; the names of the elements indicate the kinds of stressor included. The sixth source of pressure looks at the interface between work and home, picking up the pressures that people bring from home into work and those that they take home from work. Type A behaviour pattern is now a familiar construct to most readers; it was first recorded 25 years ago as the result of studies of cardiac patients, many of whom were characterised as being time pressured, ambitious etc. It is included in the OSI because of the evidence that individuals scoring high on Type A measures create pressure for themselves (and others). Perceived locus of control, in the OSI, refers largely to the individual's perception of his decision-making latitude and ability to influence aspects of his work. The OSI also includes stress coping strategies. It must be noted, however, that the six strategies included in the instrument assess the frequency of strategy use and do not necessarily imply

Table 3. Sum of pressure scores

Occupational group	Mean	Rank
Student nurses	224	1
Nurses with the elderly	216	2
Mental illness nurses	213	3
Catering staff	212	4
Nurses in critical care	211	5
Nurses in medicine/surgery	208	6
Physiotherapists	207	7
Senior nurse managers	203	8
Junior doctors	199	9
Occupational therapists	198	10
Medical records staff	197	11
Health visitors/district nurses	195	=12
MLSOs (laboratory scientists)	195	=12
Finance department staff	194	14
Midwives	191	15
Radiographers	189	16
Personal secretaries/administrative and clerical	181	17
Chiropodists	174	18
Consultant medical staff	168	19
General managers	166	20

that a strategy was appropriately selected, used skilfully or successful. The strain effects include measures of both mental and physical (ill)health and a number of measures of job satisfaction.

Results

Table 3 shows the sums of the six categories of pressure scores for the occupational groups investigated in the stress audit. The scores of the different occupational groups should be considered alongside the nine key characteristics of jobs identified by Warr.[5] The two occupational groups who are in the most senior positions in the NHS hierarchy, and have the greatest amount of decision-making latitude, report the lowest levels of pressure whereas student nurses report the highest levels. Many observers would expect junior doctors to be amongst the most stressed of NHS groups; their relatively low level in this study may be due to the lack of emphasis the OSI puts on hours worked.

Table 4. Job satisfaction scores

Occupational group	Mean	Rank
General managers	99	1
Consultant medical staff	96	2
Health visitors/district nurses	87	=3
Chiropodists	87	=3
Nurses in critical care	87	=3
Occupational therapists	87	=3
Student nurses	85	7
Midwives	84	=8
Junior doctors	84	=8
Nurses in medicine/surgery	82	10
Personal secretaries/administrative and clerical	81	11
Senior nurse managers	80	=12
Radiographers	80	=12
Nurses with the elderly	79	14
Finance department staff	78	15
Physiotherapists	77	16
Mental illness nurses	76	17
Medical records staff	74	18
Catering staff	68	19
MLSOs	65	20

Table 4 shows the strain effect total job satisfaction scores of the occupational groups. Here the general managers and consultant medical staff report the highest levels of job satisfaction whereas the most dissatisfied groups include the laboratory scientists (MLSOs), catering staff and medical records staff. Again dissatisfaction correlates well with Warr's nine job characteristics.

Table 5 shows the rank orders of the occupational groups in terms of their reported ill-health symptoms. Student nurses and nurses with the elderly reported more frequent and intense mental ill-health symptoms than other groups, with general managers and consultant medical staff the lowest levels. The OSI mental health sub-scale measures cognitive symptoms of anxiety and depression, including items on worrying and poor concentration. The physical health sub-scale looks at the somatic symptoms of anxiety and depression. Interestingly, it is the personal secretaries and administrative and clerical staff who report the highest levels of symptoms.

Table 5. Current state of health

Occupational group	Mental ill-health: rank (highest)	Physical ill-health: rank (highest)
General managers	19	18
Consultant medical staff	20	17
Health visitors/district nurses	=3	13
Chiropodists	11	20
Nurses in critical care	7	4
Occupational therapists	6	5
Student nurses	=1	6
Midwives	13	=8
Junior doctors	8	=8
Nurses in medicine/surgery	15	16
Personal secretaries/administrative and clerical	10	1
Senior nurse managers	9	10
Radiographers	16	11
Nurses with the elderly	=1	3
Finance department staff	17	15
Physiotherapists	=3	14
Mental illness nurses	5	12
Medical records staff	18	2
Catering staff	14	7
MLSOs	12	19

Table 6 shows the reported levels of sickness absence in the previous six months of the major occupational groups.

Table 6. Comparison of occupational groups on self-reported sickness absence (days in 6 months)

Occupational group	Mean	(s.d.)	Median
Administrative and clerical staff	4.6	(7.6)	1.8
Ancillary and maintenance	4.9	(6.6)	3.0
PAMs	4.6	(9.2)	2.5
Nurses	5.5	(10.7)	2.7
Doctors	1.6	(6.2)	0.7
Scientists and technicians	2.5	(3.7)	1.5
General managers	0.7	(1.7)	0.7

The health care workers in this survey were compared with health care workers in two other NHS health districts, one in the former West Midlands Regional Health Authority and another in East Anglia. The three groups were found overall to be very similar (details can be found in Rees and Cooper[6]).

The scores obtained by the Darkshire health workers were also compared with non-health care workers from a wide range of industries.[6] Health care workers reported significantly higher levels of pressure on all six indices, had lower Type A behaviour pattern scores, had a more internal locus of control, used five of the six coping with stress categories more frequently, and scored lower on the mental ill-health sub-scale. The two groups did not differ in terms of either physical ill-health or levels of job satisfaction. Thus, whilst health care workers regard themselves as being under greater pressure at work than workers in other industries, their lower Type A scores, greater decision-making latitude and use of coping strategies prevented them from having higher ill-health symptoms and lower levels of job satisfaction. In this study, caring does not seem to damage your health.

Costs of stress for the organisation

At the beginning of this chapter the costs to industry, and to the NHS in particular, of work-related stress were presented. These figures are now put into the perspective of Darkshire which may facilitate more manageable analysis.

In one financial year the organisation lost 77,248 days through sickness absence (approximately 16 days per whole time equivalent employee). The Health and Safety Executive estimate that 40% of sickness absence is stress related, suggesting that for Darkshire 31,000 days were lost due to stress, ie approximately 6 days per w.t.e. employee. This is equivalent to 134 w.t.e. staff being absent, due to stress, for a whole year. The Institute of Manpower Studies recently estimated that the average cost of a nurse's short-term absence is £70 per day (and nurses represent two-thirds of our workforce). If all our days lost to stress were short-term absences by nurses, Darkshire will have lost £2,170,000, to which must be added the other costs to the organisation resulting from poor performance, low morale, and accidents, as well as the costs to individuals and their families.

References

1. Currie D. Report, Southampton Institute of Higher Education, 1993.
2. Payne R, Firth-Cozens J (eds). *Stress in health professionals*. Chichester: Wiley, 1987
3. Bailey RD. *Coping with stress in caring*. Oxford: Blackwell, 1985
4. Jenkins R. Prevalence of mental illness in the workplace. In: Jenkins R, Coney N (eds). *Prevention of mental ill health at work*. London: HMSO, 1992
5. Warr P. Job features and excessive stress. In: Jenkins R, Coney N (eds). *Prevention of mental ill health at work*. London: HMSO, 1992
6. Rees DW, Cooper CL. Occupational stress in health workers in the UK. *Stress Medicine* 1992; **8**: 79–90
7. Cooper CL, Sloan SJ, Williams S. *Occupational Stress Indicator management guide*. Windsor: NFER-Nelson, 1988

9 | Organisational stress: strategies for management

Steve McKeown
Medical Director, Cheadle Royal Health Care Services

This chapter describes the evolution of a stress management initiative which began at ICI Pharmaceuticals in 1986 and has continued to the present day. On 1 January 1993 ICI Pharmaceuticals business became a constituent member of Zeneca Limited. Zeneca Pharmaceuticals employs 13,000 people, 4,400 of whom work in the United Kingdom. The pharmaceuticals industry is an extremely competitive business sector in which to operate and is exposed to pressures that can translate themselves into high levels of stress in individuals. It is also largely research orientated, depending on a high degree of creativity with long periods of uncertainty as to the final outcome of expensive development programmes. Such factors compound the pressure on individuals. Tight controls on costs, a high volume of new work, the drive for high quality and compliance with regulatory authority requirements and the law all make the working environment tough and demanding.

A significant proportion of the senior employees are medically qualified, and pharmaceuticals business provides a relevant and interesting paradigm to consider stress management within health care.

The chief medical officer of Zeneca Pharmaceuticals recently wrote:

> During the last few years, problems associated with stress have increasingly been a matter of concern to individual employees, to managers, to particular departments and to the personnel department and staff in the health centres.
>
> A number of individual cases of stress-related conditions were being seen by the nursing and medical staff and were being treated in a variety of ways. Some were being referred to psychiatrists or psychologists. Others were receiving treatment from their GPs.
>
> Some of these cases occurred in those parts of the organisation which were clearly under considerable business pressure. Others were working in less pressurised departments.
>
> In the mid 80s, however, the medical and nursing staff noticed a significant increase in the numbers of people coming to them for the first time with stress-related conditions. A number of

> others have talked in confidence with members of the personnel department.
>
> Managers, either individually or in group, have increasingly sought the help of the medical officers in discussing the causes of stress and how best to avoid it, and in dealing with individual cases.
>
> Until comparatively recently a major obstacle to making progress in tackling stress problems has been the instinctive feeling that admission of their existence is a sign of weakness. Individual employees have left it too late to seek help because they have thought (in many ways correctly) that to admit to suffering from stress would be considered tantamount to failure and would prejudice their career. For the same reasons managers, most of whom are relatively tough and presumably better able to cope with stress themselves, have been reluctant to admit to stress in their departments, and have been very unsure as to how to tackle it.

Stress is a necessary and integral part of life. The right amount is useful to the individual, leading to good motivation, contentment and a good use of time. Organisations and individuals with the right amount of stress are usually productive and profitable.

What is 'stress'? One observer described it as 'a reality—like love or electricity—unmistakable in experience yet hard to define'. Stress is, of course, not confined to the working environment but may be related to home life (domestic circumstances) and the social scene. 'Occupational stress' can mean either the pressure that work puts on individuals or the effect of that pressure. All work puts some pressure on individuals; in general the more demanding the work the greater the stress. The effects of this are not necessarily harmful and indeed should lead to higher output and satisfaction with work; however, a point of diminishing returns is reached, beyond which increasing stress leads to reversed effects: lowered efficiency, job satisfaction, performance and mental well-being. Chronic existence of stress at this level is known to lead to serious health problems.[1]

The number of cases known to an occupational health department will always be only the tip of the iceberg, since many patients actively wish to conceal their problems from their employer in fear of stigmatisation or career prejudice.

Zeneca Pharmaceuticals employs approximately 4,000 employees located in two pleasant, rural locations in Cheshire enjoying good facilities. Between 1983 and 1986 the number of known cases of stress-related illness rose from 23 to 90 per year. There was obvious concern within the company about the casualty rate and there was general acceptance that the organisation was experiencing high stress levels which were damaging for many individuals.

In common with most, if not all, large organisations, Zeneca personnel and medical managers received large amounts of unsolicited material relating to stress management and were also aware of the existence of Employee Assistance Programmes (EAPs). These commercially available stress management packages were incomplete, overpriced or unethical — sometimes all three. A quotation from novelist Alison Lurie is particularly relevant:

> . . . and their courses to be composed of equal parts of common sense and nonsense, that is, of the already obvious and the probably false.

Employee Assistance Programmes

EAPs are an established part of the USA employment culture. In essence they provide confidential counselling, usually on site, funded by the employer and conducted either by training in-house staff or by external consultants. The EAP industry has grown rapidly within the USA, peaking in the mid-1980s. It is a predictable and well researched activity which claims to have demonstrated good cost benefits at an American take-up rate of approximately six employees per thousand per annum. The industry has developed only patchily in the UK, originally implemented by the European divisions of American parent organisations, and more recently by a number of companies set up for the purpose. The UK experience suggests that EAPs are perceived differently by English employees who take up the service more readily, but often with social, domestic or financial problems rather than addictions or psychological distress. Traditionally, English employers have not involved themselves actively in the health care of their employees, leaving such provision to the National Health Service and latterly to private health care funded by private health insurance schemes. Every English resident is entitled to the services of an NHS family doctor without payment for a service, and the traditional EAP model does not sit comfortably alongside existing services. It also requires an initial financial commitment from employers in setting up programmes, and this is rarely easily obtained. For these and other reasons, Zeneca in common with most major UK employers had chosen not to follow the EAP model.

It is clear that many individuals are seeking psychological help, and that more and more therapists are keen to sell it, usually untroubled by their lack of registerable qualifications, quality control or safety nets in the form of onward-referral networks for those who need treatment that is either different from or more extensive than an individual therapist can provide. This trend is at best unethical, at worst dangerous, since all patients have the right to expect a thorough, skilled and broadly based assessment of their problem before being launched into a treatment programme. There is no evidence which allays concern that patients end up receiving the treatment approach most favoured by the therapist they meet, rather than that most appropriate to their need, but how many counsellors can confidently diagnose clinical depression?

Internal research

In 1986, 656 employees at an ICI site were sent copies of the 12-item General Health Questionnaire (GHQ-12),[2] through the internal mail, and invited to complete and return them in confidence. Eighty-one per cent were returned, of which 77% were usable. 'Caseness', that is positive evidence of psychiatric morbidity, was detected in 19%. The typical sufferer was male, aged 40–49 and in a managerial or administrative job. This detection rate is higher than in many other sample populations. ICI/Zeneca management consulted to draw up a list of possible stressors within the organisation which revealed the following. This list is probably applicable to many other organisations.

1. Rapid growth.
2. Increasing complexity.
3. Organisational change to meet growth.
4. Drive to become truly international.
5. Pressure to sustain high levels of profit.
6. Pressure to bring new products to market.
7. Tight control of manpower.
8. Sheer volume of new work.
9. High quality of work expected.
10. Commitment reaching a level where guilt is felt whenever work is not being done.

The project

The aims set out in Table 1 were developed for a comprehensive stress management service. A working group was set up to find ways to implement these aims.

The existing organisational management culture was essentially

Table 1. The aims of a stress management service

Aims	Staff involved
Treat casualties	Occupational health
Detect other cases	Occupational health managers
Legitimise stress	Senior management
Increase awareness	Managers Training Occupational health
Teach skills	Training Occupational health
Improve culture	Total organisation

a Type A, machismo-orientated approach to work where stress problems were usually concealed. A complex mythology declared, for example, that a good manager was able to work effectively immediately after returning from a long haul flight. A magical belief that increasing seniority should bring immunity from stress maintained these taboos.

Paradoxically, the organisation was caring and supportive towards casualties (not least because of identification) who had required treatment for depression and anxiety, but this polarisation between those who had been infected by stress and a putative majority who had not was in itself a stressor.

Some stress management consultants, and in particular training consultancies, engender a belief that the effective teaching of stress management skills abolishes endogenous depression, anxiety, chemical dependence or normal adjustment reactions. This fallacy leads to a fragmented approach to stress management without any effective safety net for those who require treatment.

For all these reasons it seemed essential as a first step that the subject of stress should be legitimised. Senior management approval and participation were sought from the outset, and also agreement that a continuation, or increase, in referrals for treatment should not be seen as a failure.

The chairman's letter

If stress management is to be effective it must percolate into the informal culture of the organisation rather than occupy the agenda of a few training sessions and then be forgotten. A pivotal step was the distribution to all department heads of a letter signed by the divisional chairman explaining and supporting the initiative. This required a great deal of 'behind the scenes' discussion and support. Not surprisingly some senior managers were threatened by the idea of employees apparently being told to work less hard and to give their family and social lives a higher priority. In some quarters there was a genuine fear that the commercial momentum of the organisation might be impaired. In fact it would appear that this was not the case, and indeed it seems likely that the reverse effect occurred, although this cannot be quantified. There is no doubt, however, that this letter and the known existence of high level working parties increased the interest, enthusiasm and compliance of all staff.

Sophisticated training resources already existed within the company. In particular, attention was paid to providing effective management training to cover the commercial, technical and managerial skills needed for effective employee performance.

The challenge, therefore, was to implement a soundly based portfolio of education and skills training with the aims of:

1. Improving the detection, management and rehabilitation of psychiatric problems.
2. Creating a culture where future problems would be recognised and managed at the earliest possible stage.
3. Teaching individuals stress management skills and the ability to monitor and manage stress levels in their colleagues and subordinates.
4. Integrating these initiatives with the existing training structure.

The chosen approach was to integrate elements of health care education with existing management and life skills training initiatives.

Any such programme requires financial resources and these cannot be obtained without effective justification. This was provided in Zeneca by the internal research study which had shown a case prevalence of 19%.

The result was a series of stress management workshops which would percolate through the organisation, from the top down. Each workshop consists of 12 to 16 participants and involves one full day off-site with a half-day follow-up 3 months later. The workshop is conducted by a clinical psychologist, a training consultant and a consultant psychiatrist.

An initial requirement was that the chairman and board of directors should participate in an early workshop; it was felt that no one should be seen as being too senior or too experienced to escape involvement. This necessitated more lobbying initially but has proved an excellent investment; there is no double message in the culture suggesting the existence of an elite of stress-free supermen.

Stress management workshop objectives

The workshops have clear objectives:

1. To raise awareness of the nature of stress, the mechanisms by which it affects physical and mental performance, and the boundary between healthy stress (eustress) and unhealthy stress (distress).
2. To provide a simple overview of psychiatric illness, its prevalence and the principles and outcome of treatment.
3. To develop the ability to recognise stress and mental health problems in oneself and others.
4. To audit and practise listening skills and counselling, as appropriate for management.
5. To teach relaxation skills and to develop a personal action plan aimed at reducing identified stress.

At the follow-up, day progress on all these areas, particularly the action plan, is reviewed.

An interesting debate centred around whether attendance at these workshops should be voluntary or mandatory. Obligatory attendance enables the unconvinced to gain exposure to workshop content without having to acknowledge themselves as stressed and allows them to maintain their criticism if they wish to. There was concern as to whether this would disrupt the workshops, but this is a problem for the workshop leaders to deal with and practical difficulties have been minimal. A coercive approach has therefore been used towards attendance.

The day comprises a mixture of didactic presentations, task focused group work and project analysis such as developing lists of personal and workplace stressors, reflecting on personal stress management strategies etc. Relaxation skills and listening skills are taught, with an emphasis on conveying core messages, such as attempting to disabuse managers of the idea that every time they listen to a problem they have an obligation to solve it or at the very least to implement some action plan. Health care workers tend to acquire active listening skills through practical experience; commercial managers rarely do.

A supplementary aim is to encourage a more critical attitude towards the purchase of health care services in industry. Many companies buy private health insurance for staff as an employee benefit, but it is not unusual for the selection of the scheme to be made by an administrator who knows nothing about the product and who is often most influenced by cost. Some insurance schemes have so many exclusions that their self promotion as 'comprehensive' is quite unjustifiable. In particular they trade on the stigmatisation of mental health care and the comfortable myth that psychiatric problems, like accidents, happen only to other people.

Similarly, many stress management packages aimed at innocent training departments suggest strongly that effective stress management, time management, leadership development or whatever will abolish mental illness among the employee group. The same proposition put in physical terms would be that if an employer provided enough gymnasium equipment then physical ailments amongst staff would disappear; the fallacy is obvious, but attractive.

Casualty management

Inevitably, clinical depression, anxiety, alcohol problems and stress disorders continue to occur, and the incidence remains much the same as before the project started.

Do the workshops produce measurable benefit?

Three separate approaches have been used:

Validation using questionnaires

It was decided in 1989 to ask participants to complete questionnaires before attending the workshop and again 3 months later. Shortly after this component was added, a second half-day was arranged as a review point at this time.

Questionnaires for this purpose had to meet the following criteria:

1. They had to be concise enough to be completed in less than 30 minutes.
2. They had to be validated for test/retest reliability.
3. Normative data had to be available.

We wished to quantify:

1. Stress — suitable questionnaires were the Occupational Stress Indicator (OSI; see Chapter 8 by Rees, this volume) and the GHQ in its 12, 28 and 30 item variants. The GHQ-30 was chosen.

2. Coping — the SAS-M (Social Adjustment Scale, modified version), Beliefs Inventory and various Locus of Control (LoC) scales were considered. The Norwicki and Strickland LoC scale was chosen.

Results

It must be emphasised that this is not a controlled study. However, questionnaire data have been collected on more than 700 employees over more than four years and the results are strikingly consistent.

Stress levels within the organisation are high normal (mean GHQ 25.2), with a consistently increasing trend. The average pre-workshop score has increased by 15% over 4 years, with noticeable increases at times of organisational stress such as the takeover threat in 1991. The distribution of scores shows a 'bulge' caused by the high scores of the subgroup who are experiencing high levels of stress at any given moment; their scores are strikingly high on occasion, and it is a chastening thought that some individuals in the workplace are admitting to more stress than patients being admitted to a psychiatric clinic. It seems unlikely that their work performance will be unaffected.

When retested between 2 and 3 months later, mean GHQ scores have fallen by 15–20%, and this improvement is demonstrated in those with normal, high or very high pre-workshop scores. This latter observation is very important, since an effective intervention needs to reach the target group rather than simply preach to the converted.

Pre-workshop assessment of locus of control reveals a strongly 'internal' average score, consistent with the culture of a science based, commercial organisation. It is these 'internal' scores which particularly predispose to stress; individual scores seem to differ amongst departments and job roles, and there was no significant change at follow-up.

Overall, the number of people presenting with stress-related illness is down. We can reasonably assume that this results from improved *earlier intervention* as average GHQ scores from the workshops held in recent years indicate increasing subjective stress levels.

Feedback

Comments from individuals attending workshops continue to be positive. Individuals report a much greater awareness of the demands placed on them and how they can best organise their work, domestic and social lives to increase efficiency and enjoyment.

Demand for places on the workshop remains high and the training is seen as part of essential management training. The workshops have also helped to identify wider training needs such as the development of improved skills in assertiveness, time management etc.

The 'Getting It Right' package has been formatted for ease of use throughout ICI and Zeneca. It has been welcomed by many other organisations, institutions, health authorities and health care providers, not only in the UK but internationally.

There is clear evidence from the data available, all of which support our observations, that:

1. Stress levels within the organisation are high.
2. Some individuals are adversely affected by stress.
3. The interventions described above, especially the Stress Management Workshops, are effective in improving symptoms and restoring function quickly.

The project continues, and a current objective is to refine and extend the assessments, preferably by including a control group.

Analysis of benefit

Traditionally much of the justification for stress management training has been based on increased subjective well-being. However, since the mid-1980s a growing body of research has demonstrated objective improvement in cardiovascular health resulting from behaviour modification, including relaxation training, as a first-line treatment for hypertension in general practice and in improving outcome for post myocardial infarct patients.[3,4]

There is also a need to evaluate cost benefit in terms of employee productivity, employee turnover and sickness and absence rates. This, however, is notoriously difficult to do with any accuracy because of the number of complicating factors which prevent the assumption of a fixed baseline.

Although the development of the project was empirical, its key aims are supported by the draft proposals established by the United States National Institute of Occupational Safety and Health in 1986, which were:

1. Attention to job design.
2. Improved surveillance.
3. Improved training, transfer of information and resource development.
4. An enriched mental health component within industry (occupational) health services.

The ICI/Zeneca Pharmaceuticals strategy was carefully thought out and was based on the following elements:

1. Early involvement of directors and general managers.
2. Collaboration between occupational health, training, organisation experts and managers.
3. Effective communication with managers regarding the importance of mental health and stress.
4. Adoption of suitable parameters to quantify the business position.
5. Introduction of well planned, professional training and educational programmes, including skills training workshops.
6. Evolution of a finely tuned, validated workshop, based around two high quality videos.
7. Effective publicity with the production of leaflets, booklets and other educational training aids.
8. A complementary counselling and treatment service.
9. Monitoring, using appropriate measures, to assess the benefits of the above initiatives.
10. Implementation of a cultural change initiative within the business leading to better development of individuals and targeting of organisational efforts to agreed goals.

In summary

Defining objectives and accountability clearly, setting priorities and managing time effectively are essential. In an innovative and demanding environment, maintaining the health of staff and managing stress positively is likely to improve productivity, reduce errors, increase creativity, improve decision-making and lead to enhanced job satisfaction.

A policy for mental health is not a stand alone initiative, but part of an integrated approach to managing a high quality organisation.

The challenge in any organisation is to allow and encourage an appropriate amount of stress or pressure, to enhance the performance of individuals, the departments where they work and thus the business and organisation as a whole.

There are persuasive reasons to believe that the approaches outlined above are equally applicable within the medical world. We owe it to ourselves, our patients and our colleagues to become more sensitive to these issues and to ensure that the educational and preventive initiatives which design and implement for others are widely available within our own work situations.

References

1. Cooper CL, Marshall J. *White collar and professional stress.* Chichester & New York: Wiley, 1980
2. Goldberg D. *The detection of psychiatric illness by questionnaire.* Oxford: Oxford University Press, 1972
3. Friedman M, Thoresen CE, Gill JJ, Ulmer D, *et al.* Alteration of type A behaviour and its effect on cardiac recurrences in post-myocardial infarction patients: summary results of the recurrent coronary prevention project. *American Heart Journal,* 1986; **12**(4):, 653–65.
4. Ornish D, Brown SE, Scherwitz LW, Billings JH, *et al.* Can lifestyle changes reverse coronary heart disease? The lifestyle heart trial. *Lancet* 1990; **336**: 129–33.

10 Doctors in crisis: creating a strategy for mental health in health care work*

Roger Higgs
Professor and Head of Department of General Practice and Primary Care, King's College School of Medicine and Dentistry

The National Health Service is not all that well, nor are many of those who work within it. Individual doctors, in common with other carers, may be at personal risk or may be more vulnerable than many, but this is also a critical moment for medicine in general, and a doctor's role and society's expectations of it are changing. A distant, paternalistic figure is not what a more consumer conscious patient group now wants or needs—if it ever did. Beyond the consultation, the relationship between doctors and the service is also rapidly changing, as paymasters struggle to control mounting costs. In the United Kingdom we have seen a completely new model of health care developed (or imposed) which has challenged many of the traditional ways of looking at the tasks of medicine, the values implicit in medical processes, and the roles of professionals. So we need to examine the health of the people working in this system. Without a clear strategy for mental health in the workforce, the health service may risk severe dysfunction or even collapse. However, diagnosis precedes treatment so we must look first at some of the reasons for poor mental health in doctors. I shall use a model that is familiar to me in my work in general practice which poses the questions in such a way as to suggest some answers.

Personal mental health problems

We know that doctors appear more likely to get depressed and to kill themselves than do equivalent colleagues in other positions. Doctors have easy access to the means of suicide but there is also consistency between the high incidence of depression and the alarming figures of alcohol and drug use and high divorce rates. All these open a small window onto the unhappiness which may exist in some doctors' families, affecting probably not only their own lives and work but also those of their spouses and children. In

*This paper is based on the Ernestine Henry Lecture, 1994

that doctors often follow their parents into the profession, unhappy families may be more important than we realise.

Perhaps most striking is the widespread unhappiness amongst junior doctors. King and colleagues reported 7 out of 10 doctors remembering previous episodes of moderate or severe emotional distress.[1] This was more common in younger doctors and in women, and was closely associated with their work. Other studies have demonstrated that between a quarter and a third of junior doctors may suffer from clinical depression.[2] A depressed patient coming to hospital has a high chance of first seeing a doctor who may be even more depressed than he or she is.

What is being done to remedy this? Doctors are being asked to work even harder, and more tasks are being assigned to them—but not, it seems, tasks that are likely to nourish the worker. Perhaps this partly explains the apparent increasing tendency for qualified medical students to give up medicine or to practise for only a short time. Equally, discussion of stress in general practice in the UK seems to have been associated with a fall in recruitment to vocational training schemes. At a putative cost of £150,000 or so to train a doctor,[3] if students do not go on to practise, there are also serious economic implications.

The model

In looking at preventable mental ill-health, it is more helpful to pursue a problem-solving approach than a classical medical or psychiatric model. We need something that can help us to look at key points where strategic intervention may be of use. A starting point is suggested by the work of Brown and Harris,[4] but modified for use in general practice in approaching patients with depression.[5] It suggests that distress may arise from a number of sources (Fig 1). A person may be particularly vulnerable, and in a difficult life or work situation. Stress may rise, and supporting relationships or coping strategies may fail. A previous experience or association may become significant, and a small event may precipitate a personal crisis. There is a school of thought within psychotherapy that such a crisis may not always be a completely bad thing. People who 'break down' may also 'break through' to a more realistic assessment of themselves or of the problems they face. But even if there is something positive for an individual to gain (with help), for the service there is clearly always something lost when a worker stops work or performs badly. We should want personal understanding to break through in other ways than this in a healthy health service.

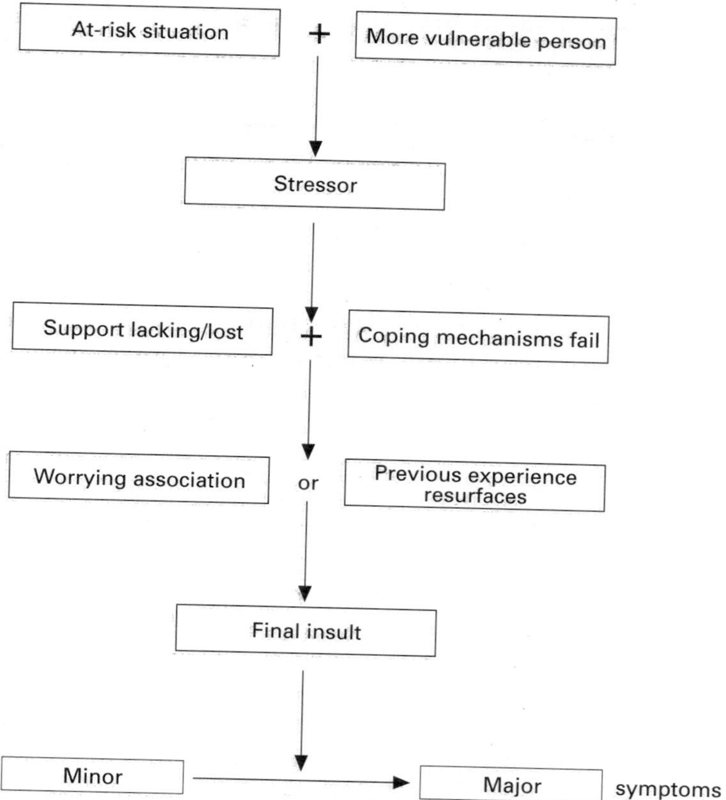

Fig 1. *A suggested example of how distress may arise from a number of sources*

Overwork and burnout

There are many risks in health care work, but structures and regulations have been created in recognition that they are needed sometimes to protect the patient from the doctor, and sometimes the doctor from the patient. Equally, the doctor or health care worker may need to be protected from himself or from the service. In the context of mental health, some of these protective features are clearly failing.

Overwork is probably the most immediate and clearly delineated problem. Extreme tiredness and in some situations sleep deprivation may be of a nature and intensity in medical work that would not be allowed in other walks of life. The current solutions proposed for junior doctors in this country, while welcome, do not seem to have addressed the roots of the problem. New rotas, which may reduce time on the wards, may not have reduced the work to be done but do seem to have diminished the opportunities for education with senior colleagues and in some cases have challenged job satisfaction. Making boundaries or limiting work is difficult in medicine, and working structures and practices often lay doctors and nurses open to the risk of abuse.

Another type of chronic tiredness which may affect doctors is chronic caring stress or burnout.[6] The literature is now large but the key features of the condition are feelings of emotional depletion and exhaustion. It has been particularly reported in general practice[7] where open access creates perhaps greater emotional demands on doctors balanced by less daily variation in work and a more flat career structure than in the hospital service.

Medical heroism

Could it be that the practice of medicine is intrinsically risky? Certainly this was the case in the past when a doctor would visit a patient with a contagious disease without protection from immunisation or chance of real cure. This must have required great courage, or the self-deception that somehow one's very profession provided protection, or that one was in some senses superhuman. Courage may be linked with blind audacity and with false ideas of being invincible or invulnerable. We recognise the attitude that leads a doctor on a ward round to open with his bare hands the wound that has been so carefully tended by nurses with aseptic technique, but it is less easy to detect the flaw in the professional who allows himself to work well past the danger point of exhaustion.

Naked courage suggests battle and heroism, and medical work is often described in terms of battle and struggle. We 'fight' an infection, the treatment may be 'aggressive' or the disease require 'heroic' measures or 'targeted' treatment and so on. The 'front-line' aspect of the work is real, and may keep doctors fighting for their patients' lives when others would give up. However, wars are won with scant regard to the detrimental effect on the battleground—in medicine this is the patient—and they reduce discussion and critical thinking. Battles sacrifice the young and fit; it is they, like our SHOs, who are in the frontline.

To be a hero is to be more than a mere mortal. 'Don't play God' is a trite prohibition which turns up regularly in debates on medical ethics but it acknowledges that doctors are often taking responsibility for decisions which go far beyond that expected of others in their work. So, for the unreflective, there are many forces leading to grandiose or overbearing behaviour. It is a short step from power to delusions of omnipotence, or at least to the belief that doctors may enter fields other than their own with as powerful an effect. They may be heroes in white coats or when on house calls but might also act as if above other mortals when making family decisions or when personal illness threatens.

The key type of all heroes in Western literature is Achilles, whose anger with his commander, Agamemnon, as the Greeks besieged Troy, was the theme of one of the great epics, the *Iliad*. Achilles provides an example of how heroism can lead not only to honour and glory but also to isolation and personal suffering. Bernard Knox expresses it well in his introduction to a recent translation:[8]

> To be a god is to be totally absorbed in the exercise of one's own power, the fulfilment of one's own nature, unchecked by any thought of others except as obstacles to be overcome: it is to be incapable of self-questioning, or self-criticism. But there are human beings like this. Pre-eminent in their particular sphere of power, they impose their will on others with the confidence, the unquestioning certainty of their own right and worth that is characteristic of gods. Such people the Greeks call 'heroes' and sooner or later, in suffering, in disaster, they come to realise their limits, accept mortality and establish (or re-establish) a human relationship with their fellow men.

Within medicine we may see some of the negative aspects of this heroism. There is the stress of isolation (clinical autonomy), the 'macho' characteristics and the ignoring of relationships with others and of the interdependence with colleagues and patients which is the way the real world works. Achilles is a good model for another reason. Near the end of the *Iliad*, he recognises his own humanity again because he is confronted at night in his tent by the old Trojan King Priam, the father of the man Achilles hated most and killed. In Priam he recognises his own father, and the son in himself, and at long last his own humanity against the heroism. There comes a point in many doctors' lives when they are forced to confront their own humanity through personal tragedy, misdemeanour or illness. We are not the only profession who climb high and whose falls are therefore traumatic, but we appear to be in a small minority among those who climb and take few precautions.

George Eliot, in *Middlemarch*, drew a contrast between her medical hero, Lydgate, who made himself vulnerable by his clinical and scientific ambitions (and his tragic choices in his private life), and the other main character, Dorothea. She came to a painful understanding of herself in her marriage with the older Casaubon:[9]

> It had been easier to her to imagine how she would devote herself to Mr Casaubon, and become wise and strong in his strength and wisdom, than to concede with that distinction which is no longer reflection but feeling—an idea wrought back to the directness of sense, like the solidity of objects—that he had an equivalent centre of self, whence the lights and shadows must always fall with a certain difference.

We may disagree as to how easy it would be to practise clinical medicine always with a strong realisation of the patient's 'equivalent centre of self' but we should not leave the area of heroism without considering the realities of power within management as well as clinical relationships. There is a warning from a modern economist for those involved in leading change. Hirschman examined the balance between private and public in economic theory, and concluded that idealism and misused power can easily go together:[10]

> A heady feeling of excitement is generated when the consciousness of selflessly acting for the public good is combined with the sensation of being free to overstep the traditional boundaries of moral conduct, a sensation closely related to power.

Lord Acton rides again: medical power, or the sensation of it, may be as corrupting as any.

Coping strategies

Among the skills that the young doctor must learn are those of dealing with the stresses and temptations of medical work. Some of these coping strategies may be of limited usefulness, some ultimately self-defeating (Table 1). For instance, doctors often appear

Table 1. Some strategies used for coping with stresses of medical work

- Ignore the doctor–patient relationship
- Don't get involved
- Keep your distance
- Don't give up
- Doctors are never ill
- Don't talk about it and they won't worry
- Stick to the medical issues

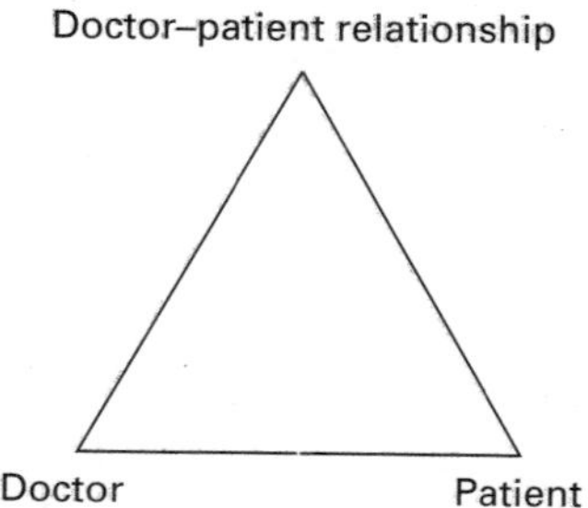

Fig 2. *The doctor–patient relationship*

to ignore the essential context of their work: the doctor–patient relationship. This is not necessarily a long-term relationship, although this can be very powerful in general practice or in working with incurable illness; it refers to the fact that doctors are with patients as soon as they begin any clinical work. This is represented as the first of a series of triangles in Fig 2. What happens between these two people is as vital as what is happening in the body or mind of the patient or the mind of the doctor.

Perhaps the importance of this is minimised because this is an area of emotional rather than intellectual work. It is here in our relationships that we may feel pain. It may be difficult to work objectively and carefully on the body of someone you love. By analogy, doctors are enjoined not to get involved with patients. However, by being distant, they do not necessarily protect themselves from the contaminating effect of pain, anxiety or depression. It may accumulate unseen. Also, as a more immediate effect a doctor who fails to recognise a patient's anxieties may also fail to make the correct diagnosis. In the long term, important harm may be done because this aspect of illness is not included in the management plan. But involvement says more about emotional distance than about recognition. The correct 'distance' between a patient and a professional in terms of their relationship is equally important but requires as skilful adjustment as any other part of the clinical care. As all the evidence from questionnaires and complaints bears witness, a doctor is not only expected to be skilful but also to be kind and to care. Objectivity is also important for both doctor and patient. There is a balance to be struck. Alistair Campbell has suggested that medical and other caring work could be seen as a type of 'moderated love'.[11] Brody, in a detailed analysis, has pointed out how much more harm may come from careless non-involvement than from the reverse and suggests that a good analogy for professional distance in medicine is the involvement we all allow ourselves in reading a gripping book or in seeing a good play.[12] Nevertheless, the skill and judgement needed to get the emotional distance correct can only be derived from practice; constant checking, adjustment and reflection are required.

Another set of rules of thumb for doctors is that they must always cope, show no weakness and never be ill. The association of illness with weakness is not only demeaning to patients but also does the doctor a disservice. One might argue that doctors cannot ever understand what it is like to be a patient or what it is like to take treatment unless they have experienced it themselves, so illness or distress may be an important teacher.

No place has yet been found for this idea in medical training; the possible reasons may be instructive. Jung suggested the existence of polarities or archetypes in human life; one of these is the healer/sufferer. Healthy people see themselves as being able to occupy positions at both ends of this polarity—to be, when ill, a patient, and, when at work and well, a healer. People whose power lies only in being ill may be no more damaged or damaging than those who see their power only in being well and in healing others. There is, in the Jungian literature, the concept of the 'wounded healer'.[13] Here we find the idea that the doctor who recognises his or her own vulnerability and can live with it is thereby a more powerful healer. This is confirmed in practice, and once more suggests that there may be beneficial aspects of distress or that distressed doctors may not necessarily be missing the point. Some may be more sensitive to real issues than colleagues, or gaining important insights which, when understood, will help them and their patients.

Such doctors are unlikely to believe our final rules of thumb that being silent on any matter will reduce anxiety, or that keeping the focus on the narrow medical issues may help everyone through an emotional quagmire. It is quite the reverse. Incurable or long-term conditions pose a particular problem for the therapeutic enthusiast. Nothing is worse than the patient who won't or refuses to get better. Professional carers may be finally driven to reveal primitive or unpleasant sides of themselves, blaming the patient, getting angry, perhaps even subconsciously wishing the patient dead. In Tom Main's moving account of working with nurses looking after incurable psychiatric illness, a clear warning is issued:[14]

> A sufferer who frustrates a keen therapist by failing to improve is always in danger of meeting primitive human behaviour disguised as treatment.

Transitions

Even if medicine is risky and its coping strategies sometimes self-defeating, most doctors negotiate their daily lives successfully. The exception may come when a change in role makes the person particularly vulnerable. This may often be seen at points of change in student life or in house jobs. Medical students appear to be particularly liable to stress.[15]

In another study, using a symptom checklist, nearly 25% of undergraduate medical students met the criteria for psychiatric diagnosis.[16] For junior doctors, the first house job poses the greatest test as a vast range of new skills have to be acquired. Junior doctors, in theory, get career guidance and teaching and support from seniors, but most studies show that for a sizeable minority these contacts are fictions; a quarter of the juniors in one study had no feedback in their performance and no career guidance.[17] Even when a career line is established, there may be similar difficult points, and becoming a specialist may face the postholder with the challenge of yet more new skills to acquire. There may be a 'seven year itch' when a doctor begins to 'run out of steam' in a post, or questions his or her long-term plans. Mid-life and retirement crises too are no less potent for being hidden amongst other changes within the health service.

Sensitising experiences

Professionals build barriers between their personal and professional lives in order to provide a consistent service. A doctor under stress may find that a previous experience, particularly powerful and therefore perhaps well hidden in the subconscious, resurfaces. Although a general practitioner avoided being raped when working alone, by skilfully talking her potential assailant out of the surgery, she could not return to work. Further exploration with her own doctor revealed that as a junior she had to stitch up the vagina of a child rape victim. This experience had been extremely distressing and she had received no help or support from her seniors. It is relatively common in working with general practitioner trainees for the trainer to find that a patient who appears to be 'difficult' has some resonances in the trainee's own private life. Michael Balint, in his important work with general practitioners, concluded that 'difficult patients' might in some ways be a product of 'difficult doctors' who had not resolved important relationships in the present or the past.[18]

Table 2. Features of post-traumatic stress disorder

- Persistent anxiety
- Irritation and difficulty in concentrating
- Sleep problems
- Avoidance of reminders/difficulty of recall

but

- Flashbacks and dreams
- Emotional numbness
- Diminished interest and increased detachment

A model that may point in the same direction is one relating to the relatively new field of post-traumatic stress disorder (Table 2). Professions involved in disaster work, such as police, nurses or paramedics, have debriefing or counselling sessions which help them to get over the damaging effect of their experiences. There has been little similar response from those managing the work of doctors and it is interesting to compare the symptoms of post-traumatic stress disorder with those commonly experienced by people who feel 'burnt-out'. This model suggests that prevention strategies are available, provided that the stress has been identified for what it is.

Personal vulnerability

When doctors break down, some others respond by suggesting that the selection of medical students should be better. If there is a link between personality, life experiences and family events then it could be argued that we should exclude those who are particularly vulnerable, but work by Johnson suggests that such experiences are absolutely key to the reasons why students wish to study medicine at all.[19] He has shown that conscious motivation does not seem to be the whole story and suggests that some students enter medicine motivated by the need to repair their own deficits: 'giving to others what one would have wanted to give (reparation for impotence) or be given (reparation for emotional neglect as a child)'. Reviewing the first idea, he suggests that a sense of impotence or powerlessness is engendered in children by early exposure to illness or death. The power of the parent to prevent these tragedies was felt to be inadequate. The child feels let down or deeply fearful, and the choice of career is an attempt to put this right. A parallel and perhaps compounding experience is where the child feels neglected or that the parents have been too distant.

It is striking how many doctors are children of doctors or other people in the caring professions. Although this may be due to role modelling it is just as likely that other factors are at work. Doctors' children report seeing dramatically less of their medical parent than the average. It would be a natural response for someone to become a patient to gain attention. Johnson produces interesting evidence that a child might respond later by choosing a helping career to repair early emotional neglect. He further developed a framework to suggest that doctors have vulnerable self-esteem and deal with that by developing a need for patients, as well as developing the emotional detachment and a denial of personal vulnerability which we have mentioned already.

Support

Vulnerable people crucially need support. We have encountered the isolating tendency of heroic medical work, and certainly doctors are not trained in how to be good collaborators. Housemen frequently report loneliness as well as overwork to be a major factor affecting their lives. The Samaritans suggest that calls from hospital juniors are surprisingly frequent, and loneliness appears to be a major factor here. Commentators have pointed out how jobs disrupt normal social support networks;[20] other busy medical work may do the same, and a middle-aged doctor may have few friends outside medical circles.

Patterns are different between the genders. Women are more stressed than men in early hospital years and significantly more depressed in early house jobs. This may be for a number of reasons, perhaps including the lack of senior female role models, conflicts between career and family or prejudicial attitudes of male colleagues. However, the general practice literature suggests the reverse is true here, it being the men who are less comfortable and the women who feel more able to balance the conflicting demands of different aspects of work and home life.[21] Professionals from minority groups are also often vulnerable. Doctors from overseas may find that the respect accorded to a high flyer from another culture or country is different from that given to someone who is seen to be filling an unpopular or low status job not taken by a local graduate.

Organisational change

Much of the work quoted above was done before the recent

massive changes in the health service. However, there has been an increasing interest in the stress of new arrangements in hospital and general practice. Doctors feel confused and their morale drops when changes that make no sense to them are introduced. The appearance of new institutions with strong marketing profiles (and sometimes Draconian suppression of any who wish to criticise the institution) makes distress more likely but the reporting of it considerably less so. 'Trust' is one of those paradoxical words and appears to be a casualty of reorganisation in many places. The organisation must be prepared to invest in training. The key is Revans' law: learning in any time of change must be equal to or greater than the change taking place.[22]

A strategy for mental health

A strategy to approach these issues is not hard to define, even though the outline is still blurred and lacks the clarity of research to confirm its value in many places. A series of activities is suggested in Table 3 and these are worth examining in greater detail.

Prevention of risk

The main thrust of any strategy to prevent ill-health must be a determined attempt to anticipate major risk and provide protective measures where that risk cannot be avoided. This entails developing within individual professionals and health care organisations, at all levels, ways of containing and reducing damaging work stress. Thought must be given to enable doctors in training to prepare not just the medical knowledge required but also the everyday work skills and attitudes that they will need at each stage of their career.

Table 3. A strategy for mental health

- Proper anticipation of risk
- Practical organisational improvements
- Proper support at points of transition
- Appropriate confidential and professional help for those in distress
- Regular reflection time for learners
- Supervision for clinicians at all stages
- Development of processes of 'internal supervision'

These are part of routine training in other fields. Medical training should ideally include practical instruction in those personal transferable skills that some find difficult, such as dealing with paperwork, writing reports and so on. However, career progress may entail loss as well as gain. A busy houseman must be prepared not only to do the job effectively but also for the loss of spare time or social work, at least temporarily, or for changes in personal schedule. Many training jobs reduce a doctor's control over work as well as personal life. At King's, my colleagues Clare Vaughan and Shirine Pezeshgi have developed a successful preparation course on these lines for final year students before their house jobs. At the very least, orientation time should be provided for hospitals and practices at the beginning of new clinical work, with space in the courses for needs of the trainees to be considered.

Practical organisational improvements have been suggested. These may include modernisation and pruning of the curriculum in medical schools, proper holidays in the clinical period of training, improved canteens and places to meet for hospital workers, with a reasonable environment for those who have to sleep overnight. On the educational front, we are just seeing the creation of proper educational contracts, which ought at least to cover the areas in Table 4, but the key to unlocking the area of mental health most probably remains an increase in the quality and quantity of reflective time throughout a medical career.

If we are correct in sometimes viewing medical work as risky, doctors as vulnerable and unprepared, motivation for the work as variable, and coping strategies as not always appropriate then much remains to be done throughout the profession.

Table 4. Most important requirements for educational contracts

- Agreed educational aims
- A named supervising consultant
- The existence of an educational plan
- Formative assessment
- Study leave
- An induction booklet
- A checklist or log book
- Protected educational time
- Satisfactory living conditions

A counselling service for doctors

Health care workers are as likely as the general population to have problems that they are unable to solve without professional help. Yet there is a huge stigma attached to the doctor who cannot cope. This means that doctors are likely to try to work through problems on their own, or turn to drink or drugs. The model of post-traumatic stress disorder suggests that work experiences may compound the need for help. There is a national system available for doctors who are very ill, and there are groups who work with addicted doctors, but the middle ground is still not covered. Doctors need to discuss problems long before they become overwhelming and shame and guilt make disclosure impossible. To be useful, such a service must be accessible, relevant, available to all, with a reasonable waiting time, and absolutely confidential. Such a service could be part of a general counselling system but experience suggests that the counsellors would need special preparation and skills.

Reflective time

Justification for the development of a reflective process throughout a doctor's career is as old as Hippocrates: 'if treatment is good, treatment after thought must be better'. The job itself has changed in many ways, particularly away from the master/apprentice model, and is now much more public, complex and multi-faceted. The newcomer is largely expected to stand on his own feet and relationships are covered by contract. There is every pressure for an organisation to get as much work as it can out of an individual but workers under pressure may respond in a routine and uncreative way, thus increasing costs for both the organisation and the patients. We have seen that narrow medical thinking is not the answer, and how therapy that is damaging may be applied when the patient refuses to get better. These are all situations where a doctor desperately needs to think with colleagues about the best way forward. This is not likely to occur unless reflection time is provided as part of work. Other helping professions such as psychotherapists, nurses and social workers have seen this process as vital, whether it be called supervision, review or mentoring (Fig 3).

In general practice training, the reflective process has been used for many years as a powerful tool in an educational plan, on both an individual and a group basis. A three-year general practice training programme includes two years in hospital posts and one

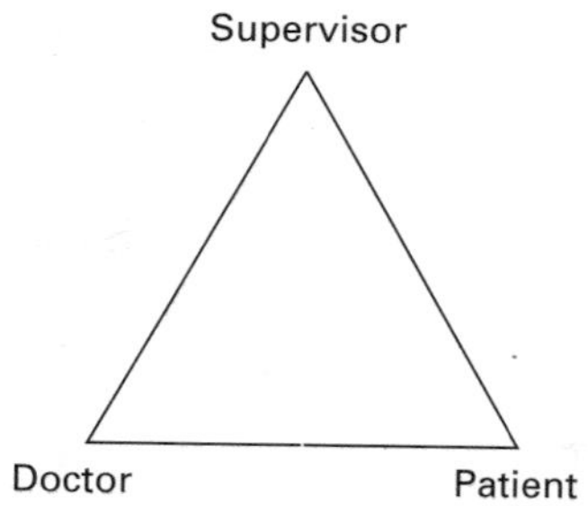

Fig 3. *The reflective process*

year in general practice. At the same time, successful courses include weekly release periods when trainees meet with a trainer, as supervisor and group leader. During the year in general practice, trainees also have individual sessions with their trainer once or twice a week which amount to between two and four hours per week. The general practice system is mandatory within the training framework; a trainer who did not offer this to a trainee would lose the training position.

A large number of learning processes occur in such contexts (Table 5). These may be approached by straightforward instruction around an agreed programme, review of consultations by video or audio tape, discussion of cases or case notes and audit projects, and open discussion of difficulties or 'hot topics' based on their importance as perceived by the trainee or the supervisor. The educational programme is negotiated between the nationally agreed curriculum and what each individual feels he or she requires.

The doctor/patient/supervisor triangle provides a safe place where a professional may examine the context within which he or she is working. Some of this may be advanced by broadening an understanding of the background of the patients, or of the complaint itself. Examples of this are provided by the public health

Table 5. Learning processes in general practice training

- Identify own feelings and manage them
- Identify and manage other sources of difficulty
- Check patient–doctor distance
- Check perceptions of others, especially patient
- Care system and colleagues

perspective espoused by Tudor Hart,[23] or the approach to everyday ethics of Campbell and Higgs,[24] but the central issue is to examine the relationship between doctor and patient, particularly when there are difficulties. These difficulties may relate to skills or knowledge but often concern feelings or attitudes. Reflection time allows the doctor to understand the personal dynamic in that relationship, and to allocate feelings, as Catherine Crowther has put it, to the right place.[25] The perspective of different people, particularly that of the patient, can be examined without embarrassment or fear. As a result, the person supervised can find the energy to begin to understand his/her own feelings, as well as managing them—and the consultation—more effectively.

Once the process of reflection has been added to the professional life of an individual, one can immediately see its possibilities. At different stages, the doctor as learner has different needs. A GP trainee may have difficulty in reaching or allocating a formal diagnosis, and an early clinical student may have trouble balancing the need to obtain information from the patient with the ideal of listening to what the patient is saying. A colleague, after working for ten years, may begin to stop caring and feels worn out. Another in mid-life facing organisational change may need help in coping with a management role while retaining a sense of independent professionalism. Thus, reflective individual or group sessions can be seen to contain management, education and personal development (Fig 4a). In formal educational terms, these link quite closely to our needs to learn in the areas of skills, knowledge and attitudes (or with 'hands, head and heart') (Fig 4b). A series of triangles can be built round these ideas to show how the three areas are related and in turn connect with other aspects of the education or training process. For instance, assessment in these areas goes *pari passu.* We need summative assessment asking whether this person can proceed on their career, formative assessment asking a creative question about educational gaps and restorative work to look at personal needs (Fig 4c). There are linked areas of work around quality control, clinical audit, personal learning and career guidance (Fig 4d).

If this is necessary, is it effective and can we afford it? Its effectiveness has been demonstrated in general practice training where we have seen rapid changes in the year currently allocated for training in practice itself. The cost depends on the methods used. A trainee or supervision group can achieve a great deal if the skills of the leader are harnessed to enable the group to tackle individual issues—supporting, challenging, reflecting, informing—but

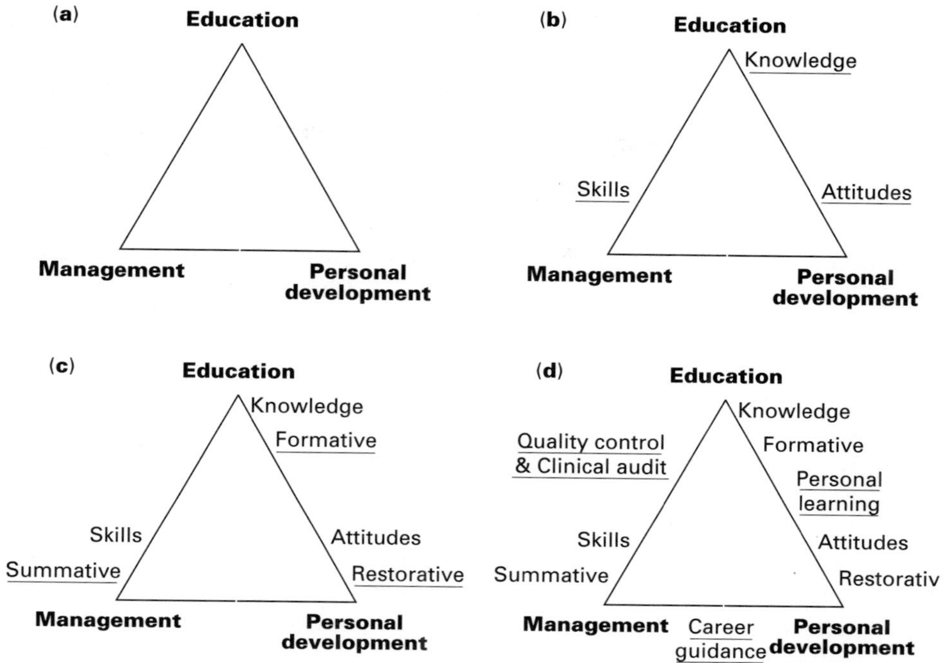

Fig 4. *(a) Contrasted learning areas for doctors in training. (b) Educational areas. (c) Assessment methods. (d) Associated feedback methods.*

some work is too personal for such a setting, and the choice of trainer, supervisor or mentor for personal work is crucial. At vulnerable career growth points, a personal tutor is probably needed, especially where there are difficulties or major changes. But these relationships should be part of the way in which our work is organised, and costed accordingly.

Internal supervision

It would be a mistake to suppose that situations requiring this sort of reflection are unusual or encountered only in training. Probably much of medical work requires it, were we able to think more carefully about the implications of what doctors are being asked to do. So ultimately a doctor needs to develop what Patrick Casement has called 'internal supervision', a process of reflection on work which is developed as a skill and does not need an outsider.[26] This is very close to what we hope to develop in ethics teaching: the internalisation of skills and approaches to checking our work, examining the values we are working to, the concerns and challenges we face, or asking the broader questions as to what is best here and what is right.[27] Doctors have to balance an enormous number of competing claims in the context of their work. None of the resources at their disposal is limitless, whether it be money for hi-tech treatments, bed-stay, nursing care, doctor time or their own enthusiasm and patience. Thus, one of the major issues to discuss is the limit or boundary of any approach, perspective or principle. Doctors must not allow themselves to be pressed beyond the boundaries of what they think is right in their work by anyone else, be they importunate patient, desperate manager, or controlling government with little understanding of the delicate ecology of health care. If we develop proper internal and external supervision, we learn many things, especially how to refuse to do too much work, provide too much treatment, do too little reflection, or change too fast with too little preparation. For healthy health care, we need real people, not stereotyped heroes. We need a new culture in which professionals look after themselves within a defined strategy which promotes their health in a practical, therapeutic and reflective way.

References

1. King MB, Cockcroft A, Goochs C. Emotional distress in doctors: sources, effects and help sought. *Journal of the Royal Society of Medicine* 1992; **85**: 605–8
2. Firth-Cozens J. Stress in medical undergraduates and house officers. *British Journal of Hospital Medicine* 1989; **41:** 161–4
3. Richards P. Personal communication.
4. Brown GW, Harris TO. *Social origins of depression.* London: Tavistock, 1978
5. Higgs R. Psychosocial problems. *Modern Medicine.* Postgraduate Partwork Series 1983; **1**:1–28
6. Maslach C. Coping strategies: causes and costs. In: McConnel EA, ed. *Burnout in the nursing profession.* St. Louis, CV Mosby, 1982
7. Winefield HR, Anstey TJ. Job stress in general practice: practitioner age, sex and attitudes as predictor. *Family Practice* 1991; **8**:140–4
8. Knox B. Introduction to Homer, *Iliad,* translated by R Fagles. New York: Penguin, 1990
9. Eliot G. *Middlemarch.* Harmondsworth: Penguin, 1965
10. Hirschman AO. *Shifting involvements, private interests and public action.* Oxford: Martin Robertson, 1982
11. Campbell AV. *Moderated love.* London: SPCK, 1984
12. Brody H. *The healer's power.* New Haven: Yale University Press, 1992
13. Guggenbuhl-Craig A. *Power in the helping professions.* Dallas: Spring, 1971

14. Main TF. The ailment. *British Journal of Medical Psychology* 1957; **30:** 129–45
15. Coles C. Learning to cope: stress and medical career development in the United Kingdom. *Medical Education* 1994; **28:** 18–25
16. Lloyd C, Gartrell NK. Psychiatric symptoms in medical students. *Comprehensive Psychiatry* 1984; **25**: 552–65
17. Garrud P. Counselling needs and experience of junior hospital doctors. *British Medical Journal* 1990: **300**: 445–7
18. Balint M. *The doctor, his patient and the illness.* London: Pitman, 1964
19. Johnson WD. Predisposition to emotional stress and psychiatric illness amongst doctors: the role of unconscious and experiental factors. *British Journal of Medical Psychology* 1991; **64**: 317–29
20. Ford GV. Emotional distress in internship and residency: a questionnaire study. *Psychiatric Medicine* 1983; **1**: 143–50
21. Cooper CL, Rant U, Faragher B. Mental health, job satisfaction and job stress among general practitioners. *British Medical Journal* 1989; **298**: 366–70
22. Revans RW. *The origins and growth of action learning*. London: Chartwell Bratt, Bromley and Lund, 1982
23. Tudor Hart J. *A new kind of doctor.* London: Merlin, 1988
24. Campbell AV, Higgs R. *In that case: medical ethics in everyday practice.* London: Darton Longman and Todd, 1982
25. Crowther C. Personal communication
26. Casement P. *On learning from the patient.* London: Tavistock, 1985
27. Higgs R. Can medical ethics be taught? In: Byrne P, ed. *Medicine, medical ethics and the value of life.* Chichester: John Wiley, 1990

RCP REPORTS

Setting priorities in the NHS — A framework for decision-making (1995)

Alcohol and the heart in perspective: sensible limits reaffirmed (1995)

Incontinence — Causes, management and provision of services (1995)

Provision of wheelchairs and special seating: guidance for purchasers and providers (1995)

Psychological care of medical patients — Recognition of need and service provision (1995)

Treatment of adult patients with renal failure: recommended standards and audit measures (1995)

Clinical audit scheme for geriatric day hospitals (1994)

Ensuring equity and quality of care for elderly people: the interface between geriatric and general internal medicine (1994)

Geriatric day hospitals: their role and guidelines for good practice (1994)

Good allergy practice (1994)

Homelessness and ill health (1994)

Part-time work in specialist medicine (1994)

Quality control in cancer chemotherapy: managerial and procedural aspects (1994)

Stroke audit package — produced by the UK Stroke Audit Group and the Royal College of Physicians (includes software) (1994)

Sleep apnoea and related conditions (1993)

Staff grade doctors: towards a better future (1993)

Reducing delays in cancer treatment — some targets (1993)

Allergy: conventional and alternative concepts (1992)

A charter for disabled people using hospitals (1992)

High quality long-term care for elderly people (1992)

Smoking and the young (1992)

Preventive medicine (1991)

A complete list of reports and other RCP publications is available from:

Publications Department, Royal College of Physicians
11 St Andrews Place, Regent's Park, London NW1 4LE

RCP PAPERBACKS

Nutrition in child health (1995)

International developments in health care —
A review of health care systems in the 1990s (1995)

Travel-associated disease (1995)

Psychiatric aspects of physical disease (1995)

Current themes in allergy and immunology (1994)

Regulation of the market in the National Health Service (1994)

Professional and managerial aspects of clinical audit (1994)

Management of stable angina (1994)

Access to health care for people from black & ethnic minorities (1993)

The role of hospital consultants in clinical directorates (1993)

Rationing of health care in medicine (1993)

Analysing how we reach clinical decisions (1993)

Current themes in rheumatology care (1993)

Measurement of patients' satisfaction with their care (1993)

Referrals to medical outpatients (1993)

Violence in society (1993)

Health systems and public health medicine in
the European Community (1992)

Measures of the quality of life (1992)

Current themes in diabetes care (1992)

Accidents and emergencies in childhood (1992)

Pharmaceutical medicine and the law (1991)

Paediatric specialty practice for the 1990s (1991)

A complete list of RCP publications is available from:
Publications Department, Royal College of Physicians
11 St Andrews Place, Regent's Park, London NW1 4LE